The Space
That
Keeps You

The Space That Keeps You

WHEN HOME BECOMES A LOVE STORY

JEREMIAH BRENT

HARVEST

An Imprint of WILLIAM MORROW

To Nate,

You cracked life open
with youre love.

and to Poppy and Oskar.
Our dream, Our truth, Our
Miracles. Home for us
will always be anchored
in your arms.

Contents

Intentions

This isn't supposed to be a pretty design book.

It's an emotional design book. Instead of being about what is obviously beautiful, it's about what is weird and thoughtful and special to the people who love it most.

The idea of home is something I think about all the time—not just the aesthetics of a house, but what makes a home that people stay with. That's something I never had and always wanted. Throughout my adult life, I lived in so many places, and they all turned out to be temporary. Ten years into our relationship, Nate and I had moved ten times. I started to wonder: What was wrong with us? Were we broken? Why couldn't we just stay anywhere? I wanted to understand what it takes to fall in love with a space, because my fantasy was to truly come home.

The idea to write *The Space That Keeps You* was born in Oprah's dining room in her home in Montecito. Oprah is a dear friend, as well as one of those people who has discovered her forever place, which you will be invited into in just a few pages.

We were sitting together and talking about home and connection and falling in love with a place, and she said, "You should write a book."

I said, "I'm just really interested in the space that keeps you. I want to know why some people never leave."

She looked at me and said, "That's your book. That's what you need to write."

And here we are.

A home is a kind of living organism. It has an energy. Where does that energy come from? What is it about a space that keeps people? As someone who has longed for a space that holds me for years, I wrote this book to try and understand.

I'm just so curious about the why.

Another catalyst for this very personal exploration occurred in 2019, when Nate and I moved out of our house in Los Angeles with the kids to go back home to New York City. I had feelings about moving, but not about leaving anything in that house behind. I didn't care about the pretty things, the mantle or the decorative objects. What I would miss the most were the rituals and ceremonies that we would leave in that house, like the dance parties we had with the kids around the kitchen island every morning and evening. I've spent my whole career helping people make their homes look beautiful, and I started to wonder how much design makes people want to stay.

We all relate to ideas of home in different ways, and my husband and I are a perfect case study for this. The physical objects in our homes mean a lot to Nate, who always has so many memories tied to them. For me, it's the house itself that holds the memories. The things inside a home can go with you anywhere, but what has happened within those walls remains contained there. Those moments only echo there.

When I imagined *The Space That Keeps You*, I was curious about what motivates people who stay, who return, who put down roots and spend their lives tending to the vines. What captivated me is not how structures look, but the energy they contain. I'm obsessed with things that last. I'm fascinated by the kind of people whose grandchildren visit the home that they raised their children in. I wanted to understand, through connecting with these people and hearing their stories, what it is about a house that holds you.

Some of the people you will meet in this book have been dear friends of mine for many years; others are newer connections whose spirit and perspective move me. All of them have a relationship to home that is rich with life and story: Oprah's Promised Land, and the trees she calls the Apostles; the children honoring their parents' legacy of art and architecture in their house in Mexico; the West Village couple who emblazoned hearts on the beams within their walls; the family that runs the first Black-owned winery in Napa; the count who married a princess and figured out how to save his family's storied Venetian palazzo; the New York City gallerist who fell in love with a farm in the Portuguese country; the family who found a home that embraced them and made them feel safe and nurtured; the chef who has lived in the same apartment on the same cobblestone street for more than 40 years; the dancer who left the home where she raised her son, now grown, in order to cultivate a new piece of herself. Through visits and conversations, I got to see their spaces through their eyes and understand what they love so much about their homes. What I saw changed me.

The first and final chapters of this book are about as personal as it gets. Over the course of writing, Nate and I moved back into the first home I ever fell in love with, a wholly unexpected piece of the puzzle, which you are invited to visit in the opening chapter. After a year of conversations with the people in this book about their homes, immersing myself in these ideas, something even more unexpected happened. We bought a home in Portugal, in the kind of place that I never dreamed would be ours, which you will see in the closing chapter of this book. For me, it is the ultimate fairy-tale ending, a twist that was only possible because of this journey and what I learned along the way.

I used to think that design was the most important thing in the world. I thought it could change your life. I still think it can, to some extent. Good design is design that makes you feel something, and at its best, it bolsters the moments that matter. I love what I do, and it's my favorite thing in the world, but so much of design right now is transactional. It's too immediate. Something is missing, and it's time for the approach to change.

I wrote this book because I was curious about the houses that become more than a transaction, that become a love story, and I found what I was looking for. The twist of this design book is that design only goes so far. What really makes people stay in a home is the emotional life that emerges within the space that keeps you.

First Love

NATE AND JEREMIAH

The first space that really felt like home to me was the apartment that Nate and I lived in on Fifth Avenue when I was twenty-nine. Set on top of a building, it's the perfect marriage of space and place, like a little house that is still connected to the city. I would get home and be able to look out at New York City. I could see the most beautiful pink sunsets, and the most beautiful pink sunrises.

Nate knew that there was something really special about it right away. My husband always says that he likes an elevator ride where you press the button for the top floor. The home felt like a destination. It was a marker of success, an arrival.

Nate has told me that, before we met, he used to walk around this neighborhood and look up at these grand, old, aged, white-glove buildings, and ask himself, "I wonder who lives on the top of all of those?"

When we saw this place, he realized that the answer to that question was *us*, and that meant so much to both of us. It was the first place we ever renovated together. We weren't married, we didn't have kids yet. This act of building a home together was the first major thing we had ever gone through as a couple.

In Nate's words, "It was a real project with each other for each other. It was the beginning of our education with each other. It opened up a lot of trust and a lot of admiration from both sides."

We were so happy there. I wrote my wedding vows on the table outside, on the terrace in that house on Fifth Avenue. That place was the culmination of everything at the same time: the realization that we could have a great love, a beautiful home, and someday even a family. The realization that we could live this way.

When I asked him about his memories of that era, Nate talked about the moments when we were still waiting for Poppy to be born, and we were standing in the little room that we had crafted for her. "Opening her little closet doors, which are now our home-office doors, and seeing all of her little shoes and all of the little dresses, and knowing that in all the little drawers were all the little things, and the only thing missing was this little person."

JN 9/19/17

WELCOME HOME BABY.
WE MISSED YOU

It was the beginning
of our education
with each other

Living in that house was this blend of everything that I had ever fantasized about, and never thought was possible. I always felt so safe there.

When we left, it was to move to Los Angeles to be closer to family. It was the hardest thing I'd ever done. I'll never forget leaving the house on Fifth Avenue. Moving in had been the best day of my life. Moving out was one of the worst. For a long time, I couldn't talk about that apartment without weeping. It was like the love that got away.

In a very strange twist of events, the little house on Fifth Avenue—our first home—became ours again while I was writing this book, nearly ten years after we first said goodbye. I had spent seven years trying to get it back. By the time we did, I had been thinking about the idea of home for so long. I write these words from the first home I ever loved, the home we live in again now, in the very spot where I crafted my wedding vows.

• • •

I've always been obsessed with the way people live. My fascination with homes began when I was a child growing up in Modesto, California. On the weekends, my mother, Gwen, and I would go on home tours, checking out the open houses for homes we could not afford, and I would fantasize. Who would live there? What would they do in the home throughout the day?

My mom was a single mother who worked three jobs, the hardest-working person I've ever met. Her father had been in the Air Force, so she was a military brat. As a child, her family was always traveling, always moving.

Perhaps because of that, her sense of home wasn't rooted in a space, but in the pride that she took in making sure that our home was well taken care of. When I was in middle school, we left a questionable neighborhood and moved somewhere nicer. My mom was making good money, finally. She had worked so hard to get us to this place where we would have stability and safety. I'll never forget that move, particularly what it meant for my mother.

We stayed through high school, and then I moved to Los Angeles to figure out what to do next. From then on, I was always moving. When I was single, I moved around all the time because there was never a home that I cared about. Many of them were beautiful, but I was never home in a way that mattered. Not until Nate and Fifth Avenue.

My introduction to design as a career was purely accidental. I was an eighteen-year-old kid in Los Angeles, trying to figure out what I could do, I would find second-hand pieces at the Goodwill or on the side of the street and remake them for myself. When people came over to my house and saw those pieces, they would ask about them. My friend Fatima, whose Ojai home I invite you to experience in Chapter Ten, was one of the first people who ever asked me to make something for her. As more people started asking me to make furniture for them through word of mouth, I started charging. From there, it became, "Would you design a room?" "Would you design a couple of rooms for me?"

I worked anywhere I could get a job, from bars and nightclubs to furniture stores. Then I struck gold, with an opportunity to work with Rachel Zoe. Working as a stylist's assistant was not always the most glamorous, but I worked my ass off and I loved it.

The job led me to a personal revelation. I may have had millions of dollars' worth of fashion and jewelry at my fingertips, but that's not where my attention was. We were at a shoot and I realized that all I really cared about was the Royère sofa that the model was sitting on.

Rachel saw it too. I was in her house in Beverly Hills, soon after my moment with the Royère, when she turned to me.

"You shouldn't be a stylist," Rachel said. "You should be doing design. That's what you care about. You're so good at it. You have to do what you're passionate about."

She was right, and so I left my job with her to chase a dream and bet on myself. In 2012, I sold everything I owned—my car, my clothing, all my furniture—so that I could start my design firm. I designed a logo and put it on a decal that cost me $99, and I put it on the wall. I hired my first person, Beth, my new design assistant. I didn't know how I was going to pay her, but I knew I was going to figure it out.

A few months later, I flew out to New York to help Rachel with something and went to a party that night. That was where I met Nate, whose talk show had just ended. He was already very successful and his lifestyle was very comfortable, and I didn't want him to know that I was struggling.

Scraping together what pennies I could, I started to fly to New York every Friday to spend the weekend with Nate. There were a lot of Jack in the Box, 99-cent menu dinners; let's just put it that way.

Starting my firm, falling in love with Nate: it all happened at the same time.

Nate's connection to spaces has always related to the beauty of the home. He is drawn to bringing homes back to life or highlighting historic architecture, which is why he's just never been interested in new homes and new architecture.

His mom is a designer, and he was always lugging her wallpaper sample books from the trunk of her car to her home office. He was always surrounded by fabric samples and stone chips and wallpaper pieces. As he put it, "Our house was full of ideas."

When I asked about the homes that moved him in his youth, he told me about a trip he took with his parents when he was about eleven to visit friends of theirs—a painter and a physician—who had moved to Fargo, North Dakota.

"I remember pulling up," said Nate, "and whoa! It looked like Bruce Wayne's house. It was gabled and old and beautiful."

The home was a 1920s massive Tudor with all of the original details, one of the stateliest houses in town in the old, leafy, fancy part of Fargo. That was the first house that Nate fell in love with, but it wasn't until he was in his twenties that he experienced a moment of arrival in a space that could be his.

In 1999, Nate went to see a Chicago apartment that had been renovated in the 1940s by the architect Samuel Marx for the Block family, who owned Inland Steel. All the oak paneling in the library was Marx's own design, as were the fireplaces, and Nate loves Marx's work. When he first saw the apartment, no one had lived in it for ages. It was unfurnished, but there were still a couple of architectural elements designed by Marx, like a parchment bookshelf that stretched the full span of the living room. He knew it was meant to be his. The issue: it was way out of his budget.

Our House was full of ideas

Nate reached out to a dealer in New York City who had written a book about Marx and explained the situation.

"I want to buy this apartment but I can't afford it," he said.

She said, "Are you standing in the Block apartment in Chicago?"

"Yes."

"There are two things we can sell, the mirror and the bookshelf."

She put them in the Winter Antiques Show in New York. The money he earned from selling those pieces took care of his down payment.

Nate loved that apartment. It was a milestone for him to have a full floor in a 1920s building with an elevator that opened directly into his home. There was no central air. It had an original kitchen with metal cabinets, which he painted army green, and original countertops. The appliances in the apartment were

BECAUSE YOU HAVE HAD
MONTH
BECAUSE
THINK

NO
ONE
LOVES
OU
RE
AN
E.

LOVE

MOST

new, but the rest of it needed a lot of care, which Nate accomplished on a "major shoestring budget." He was so proud of it.

In his words, "I was in my twenties. It was incredible. I had room after room after room."

That home contained so many beautiful moments for him, but his feelings in the space changed after his partner Fernando died in the tsunami in Sri Lanka in December of 2004. Nate and Fernando traveled there together, but only Nate came home. When he arrived back in Chicago, his parents, who had been divorced since he was two, were waiting there for him with a psychiatrist. The psychiatrist came to the house every two days to talk to him alone in the library with the door closed. He couldn't get out of bed for weeks.

"We left that house together," he remembers. "The woven photographs which had been hanging in the entry were given to me two days before we left. To come home and have those hanging, and just to keep passing them, back and forth . . ."

After Fernando's death, the building was swamped with reporters wanting to talk to Nate about it, and swamped with people bringing flowers and notes and cards. Experiencing it all up on the eighth floor, Nate felt "protected, but alone. More alone than I had ever been in my entire life."

A place of joy and contentment came to embody those feelings of solitude and grief and mourning.

My husband is someone who holds on—to people, to places, to memories, to objects that are meaningful to him. It took a long time for him to let the apartment go.

My Heart loves Your Heart

It's not easy to articulate how much Nate means to me; he's everything. Many people think his superpower is his designer's eye, but I know that his real superpower is that he sees people the way they want to be seen. He's spectacular in that way.

The first place Nate and I shared was an apartment in the West Village, but that place always felt more like his than ours. Fifth Avenue was ours together, the place where we got married and became parents. We lived in the house for two years, until events in our lives shifted our perspective on where home could be. Nate's father was dying. At the same time, my father was in a coma because of an accident.

Nate wanted to move back to California, where all of his brothers and sisters live. When he said, "I just want to be around my family right now," of course, I agreed. Leaving was hard for both of us.

Nate found a house in LA for us to rent until we could buy a place. When he sent me the listing, he said, "I really love this house. Can we go look at it?"

Imagine the look on my face when I realized which house he was referring to! It was the very same house that Rachel Zoe had lived in when I worked for her and she told me that I should become a designer.

Moving into Rachel's old house was a powerful "you are capable" moment. I had last been in there as her assistant, imagining a major career change. I was coming back to LA with a daughter, a husband, and a design firm. I remember Nate holding my hand and saying, "Look what life is now. Look what we have now."

We tried loving that house, but it was not for us. Everything inside was great, but when we walked outside into the neighborhood, we just could not connect. We love having a feeling of community, and Los Angeles didn't offer that in the way New York did. There was no vibration. I had an attachment to New York; the city always felt like home to me. It was the only place where I felt like I was part of something. I fantasized about returning until the day that we packed up and moved back east.

When we returned to New York, we immediately thought about Fifth Avenue. Nate and I had discovered so much about each other in that home, so much about who we were as a couple, both good and bad. Creating that home was the first thing we did together, before anything else. To me, it was the one that got away.

We tried to buy it back, but we couldn't afford it, so we moved to another apartment in the West Village. We lived there for two years. Then we got an email from the Fifth Avenue broker saying, "It's available."

Not only did we get it back, we got the apartment beneath it too, and we've been able to come home in an even bigger way. When we first moved there, I felt like a baby. Nate was very successful and I couldn't afford to contribute financially—all my contributions were creative. This time, we were equal. This time, we needed me. It's a symbol for me of growth, of family, of partnership, of love.

Nate and I sat down to talk about our ideas of home. When I said the word "home" to Nate, what came to his mind is family. Snack drawers. A stocked refrigerator. Diaper pails. That last one surprised me, because we hadn't had a diaper pail in years. He explained it to me: the time when we had diaper pails was when this idea of home was defined for him.

"It comes from us being together, and then deciding to create a family and housing that family within the four walls," he said. "It isn't possible for me to define home without you. I don't think that that exists for me."

The home we have created on Fifth Avenue is one that supports all the different pieces of our lives—our family, our personal lifestyles, and the social parts of us.

"Who are you in this home?" I asked Nate.

"Part of me is just a super comfortable, kind of goofy dad, and incredibly relaxed the minute I walk through the door," he said. But he also appreciates order. It's important to him to know where everything is, what's inside every drawer and closet. That matters to him. Having a perfectly organized linen closet, or reaching for something and knowing where it is—that makes him feel at home.

"The other side is the persona that people have seen publicly," he added. "I love welcoming our friends into this house, I love setting up cheese and crackers, I love making drinks. I really do feel like this house is such a true representation of the two of us—how hard we work, where we've been, where we aspire to be."

For me, the house has the echoes of our time there in the past, but it really came to life when we moved back in and everybody had a place. I remember very much the second that the kids' floor was finished and they were in their rooms for the first time. All of a sudden, the house felt like somebody had turned the lights on.

As we worked on our renovation for the Fifth Avenue apartment for the second time, Nate and I kept saying to each other, "Wait a minute. Are we going to like this in twenty years?"

We had never had those conversations around anything that we'd designed before because we had never lived anywhere more than two years. Renovating this house again was something very special for us, like stepping back into our dream life.

That house on Fifth Avenue has witnessed so much pain and joy. It witnessed the death of Nate's father, which is probably the most complicated and saddest event that has happened while we were there. And, in Nate's words, it has held "a vibration of unspeakable joy that I never anticipated."

I feel the same way. We initially imagined bringing one child home here. We moved back home with two. I keep envisioning the stairs carrying our children up and down as they grow. That their rooms can change as they get older, but that kitchen island will always be the anchor for important conversations, dance parties, and birthday celebrations.

I keep wondering to myself, "Is this finally the space that keeps you?"

I don't know. The beginning is only the beginning, and only time will show us what forever looks like. All I know is that I feel really complete. When I stand in my kitchen, I'm reminded of my family's beginnings. This space housed all that. This space keeps the beginnings and more.

I feel like we have moved home.

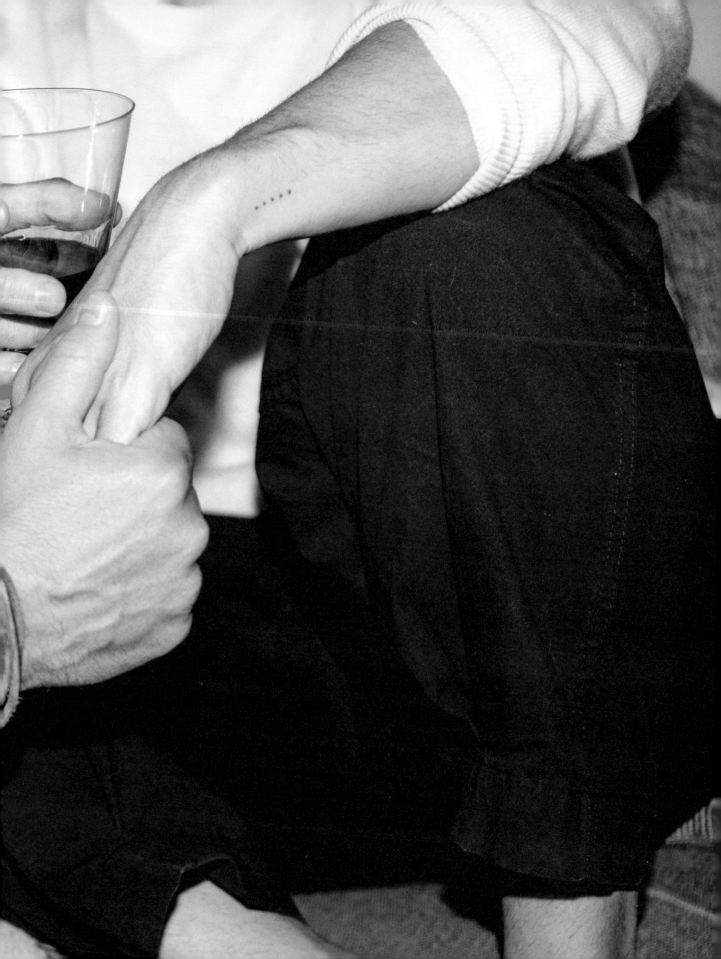

CHAPTER TWO

The Six-Tree Dream

OPRAH

Oprah is everything you think she will be: compassionate, kind-hearted, wickedly funny—she feels instantly familiar and divine in a way that can only be described as abundant. A woman who has made her way in this world, she can live anywhere she wants, in whatever settings she chooses—and she has lived in many beautiful places.

I reached out to Oprah because I wanted to talk to her about the home she calls "The Promised Land," a home that is so emblematic of who she is and what she values.

The Promised Land is in Montecito, California, a place Oprah discovered during a photo shoot for *O Magazine* in 2002. She was riding in a convertible in a Versace scarf, with the wind blowing and plenty of time to take in the street and the abundance of trees. Trees, everywhere she looked. Beyond the walls and gates that concealed the homes, even more trees. And Oprah loves her trees.

She called Bob Greene, a dear friend of hers, who was touring the country for six months with his fiancé, Urania, looking for the best places to live.

"I was in this place called Montecito," she said. "They had all these unbelievable trees and—God, what an incredible place."

"We're there right now," said Bob.

By incredible coincidence—or providence—he had just arrived in Santa Barbara, just down the road from Montecito.

Two weeks later, they were out there looking at properties. Oprah liked every house she saw, including the "Chipmunk House," which had been owned by a man whose father had created Alvin and the Chipmunks. She thought it was fantastic—eight acres, fully an "I've arrived" moment. But Bob knew there was one more potentially great home to see.

They pulled into the last home and Oprah looked up at the front lawn. That was it for her.

"It was love at first sight, baby," she said. "It was an instant. It was a whole, literally, 'Holy shit' moment."

The house wasn't even done yet; the framing had been put up and the pillars were there, but there were no floors or walls. All she cared about was the lawn—until she got out back, and saw the view of the ocean, which included the Channel Islands.

This was meaningful because, a year earlier, she had been in her penthouse on Fisher Island in Florida, a place with ample views of the ocean. Oprah loved that ocean view, but it was so vast, so connected to the sky that she could barely discern the horizon. From her bedroom, she felt like she was on the bow of the boat. What she needed was something to ground her. So, she stood on her balcony and had a conversation with the universe about it: "God, thank you very much for the ocean. But I need something to break up the ocean."

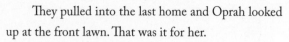

My wish for you
is that you continue
to be who and how you are
to astonish a mean world
with your acts of kindness

To ignore no vision
which comes to enlarge
your range
and increase your spirit
to dare to love deeply
and risk everything
for a good thing

Specifically, she wanted something to help her distinguish between the ocean and the sky—a rock, an island, some trees.

There in Montecito was exactly the view she had imagined.

"I laid claim to it in my spirit," said Oprah, "in my heart of hearts, the moment I walked out onto that balcony and I saw the vision that I'd held a year before."

What Oprah asks for, she receives.

• • •

When I asked Oprah about her dreams of home, she talked about her childhood hopes for a place that would fully support her. She recalled the landscape around her grandmother's house in Mississippi, the house she lived in when she was a young child, a house that was surrounded by trees, with a dirt road. This image still comforts her and calls to her.

That image is why, when she was choosing titles for her book club, she was always drawn to books whose covers featured a house and a dirt road. The way she saw it, "Got a house and a road! Must be good!"

I laid

to it in my

claim
spina

Thinking back, she laughs in the way that only Oprah can. "Nobody caught on!"

She moved at age six to live with her mother, inhabiting a "series of bad walk-up spaces," whatever they could find and afford while living on welfare. As a young teenager, Oprah went to live with her father, where she had her own room for the first time.

When she saw his house, she cried.

"Finally, I'm going to have a home," is what she was thinking. "A brick home, a real home."

On Sundays, she would travel with her father to "rich white people's neighborhoods" to admire the grand houses that were there, and she began to build fantasies about how she wanted to live someday. They saw Tudor homes and they saw homes with Georgian architecture. Although she couldn't have told you back then that it was Georgian, she knew what she liked.

"I'm going to build you a house on a hill someday," she told her father.

What she longed for most were lawns and porches and great expanses of green.

For a long time, Oprah's dream was to live in a beautiful home, surrounded by gorgeous things.

When she got a job in Baltimore, she gave her first paycheck to a decorator, excited to spend that $1,000 to create the kind of space she had long dreamed of inhabiting. The decorator disappeared with her money, and Oprah got nothing back for it, not even a curtain to hang.

Oprah still wanted her place to look beautiful, so she did her best. She wanted art for the walls but she couldn't afford "real art," so she framed posters and postcards from art museums. She acquired a single Queen Anne chair from Pier One.

As Oprah grew her career, the world began to open her up, and her ideas about what was possible expanded.

One afternoon, she went to visit her friend Arlene, a producer in Baltimore, who was married to a very prominent lawyer. Oprah pulled up to their driveway and saw a row of luxury cars out front—Jaguars, BMWs, Mercedes.

"Whoa, Arlene is rich!" she thought.

She had never encountered wealth like this before.

It was only when she was in the kitchen with Arlene, looking out the window at a row of trees, when something clicked in her mind. She didn't care about the Jaguars. She didn't need a row of cars. What Oprah wanted for herself were those trees.

She counted them: there were six trees. Like her trips to see the grand houses on the weekend with her father, her visit to Arlene's inspired her and awoke her to what was possible. She calls it her "six-tree dream."

Soon after Oprah moved into the pool house at The Promised Land, a guest on her own property as the main house was being built, she was standing in the kitchen, waiting for the tea to brew. She looked out the window, and there she saw them. Just outside, she counted six trees, just like the six trees at Arlene's house. Oprah walked outside, right up to the six trees that she could see through the window. Beyond them were thousands more.

"The thing that I'd most asked God for—'God, I need some trees. I need some trees.' And then I got them, in ways I never imagined," she said. "This is what I know. This is what I always come back to: God can dream bigger than you can dream for yourself."

The house in Montecito took four years to be completed.

Even living in the pool house, she felt embraced there. "You walk outside, and there's that ocean and the trees," she told me, "I felt it immediately."

She designed the house in the taste she thought a wealthy person was supposed to have, with real art instead of framed posters. Her idea of beauty came from other people's homes and magazines, and she asked her designer for a Louis XV style. As years went by, her taste evolved. She called another designer, Rose Tarlow, to make some changes.

When Rose saw the interiors, she said, "This is like a museum. What is this?"

Instead of mimicking someone else's style, Rose asked Oprah to think about what she really wanted in her space and describe it in one word.

"What is your word?" Rose asked her.

Oprah answered, "Books." In that moment, a house full of books was what felt most personally meaningful to her.

Today, Oprah grounds her homes in whatever makes her feel comfortable. She likes neutrals. She doesn't like more than three colors in a room—four, max. She doesn't like a lot of bright things bringing attention to themselves. She wants to feel soothed, and she wants her guests to feel the same way. She is not so attached to the interior space as much as she is to that which surrounds it, and which is surrounding her.

It is amazing and beautiful to me that the woman who has always loved trees has the largest private estate of sequoias in the Santa Barbara area. She is a loving steward of the trees and of her land, familiar with its most sacred spots.

She has a special relationship with an area on her land where twelve oaks form their own oak hammock and grove. Oprah calls them The Apostles. It is in this outdoor space that she has her prayer table and her symbols of religion: the Buddha, the angels, the crosses.

She meant to have her ashes placed here someday, under a particular huge oak, a majestic tree that formed a tunnel with another tree. After a heavy rainstorm that caused flooding, the oak uprooted and fell over. When it fell, the whole space changed for her; now she wants her ashes sprinkled in her house on Maui, another place where she keenly feels her connection to the earth and the stars.

She was so connected to that specific tree and she felt the loss of it deeply. She is trying to replace the oak with a younger tree, but that feeling of a tunnel just isn't there.

Now she worries for the rest of her trees. When wildfires sweep through the area, it is the trees on her land—"the thing you can't get back"—that she is concerned about, not the house.

"You can rebuild the house," Oprah said. "But you can't rebuild a 200-year-old oak."

Oprah has achieved her dream of having a beautiful home, and in fact, she has many. What they all have in common is the way they connect her to the sky, to the mountains, to the ocean, to the trees. It is not the houses themselves but the landscapes that hold her. She is at home when she is embraced by the mountains, the ocean, and the trees; when nighttime falls she lives in a world of pure stillness, beneath a dome of stars. In these settings, she feels like her life has been set inside a painting, like she has stepped into a dream for herself.

Nature is always her sacred space. That is where she is most fully herself, most fully connected to all beings. In nature, she is a part of everything.

My interpretation, from my time spent with her in Montecito, is that nothing inside the house really matters to her: what really matters is the trees and the landscaping. Her fantasy of always looking out and seeing a grove of trees, that's luxury to her.

In Oprah's dream of home, every window has a window seat.

"I'm the girl that has to have a room with a view, that's for sure," she said. "The view has to give back. The view has to feed you. I'm nurtured and supported and literally fed by my spaces."

That is how I imagine her, with her faced at a window, watching the clouds roll by over a grove of trees.

You can rebuild a house but you can't rebuild a 200-year-old oak

CHAPTER THREE

Accidental Paradise

DAGMAR, COSMAS, AND DEGENHART

This artists' haven in Mérida, Mexico, was built to show off. Viewed from the outside, it is a blank space. Open the doors and you enter a complete experience on the inside, a creative representation of James and Alexandra, the beautiful spirits who made this masterpiece of a maze. Every corner has something unbelievable. It is a house that was meant to be experienced.

James and Alexandra were two of my favorite humans. In 2020, they died in a tragic car accident. I was always captivated by them, and how they were so loving, so intentional. That way of being is reflected in their house and the way they related to their house. James was a prolific artist who worked with various materials, including ceramics and painting. The house is full of his work and his art studio, where Alexandra published their literary magazine, *Carpe Diem*, is just down the street.

After the loss of their parents, James and Alexandra's three children Dagmar, Cosmas, and Degenhart didn't want to sell the house. All three have taken over James's art legacy, and they are the willing stewards of their parents' vision. They don't live in the home; they are its guardians and protectors. For them, the house is an altar.

James's and Alexandra's energy is so imbued in these walls that their children cannot imagine somebody else living there. There is no space for another's energy.

Dagmar and Cosmas had a long talk with me about their feelings about this place. When they were considering what to do, Dagmar told me, her perspective was, "We either keep it forever or we burn it to the ground."

Part of the impetus and inspiration for this book came from the many conversations I had with James and Alexandra about their experience of home. When I spent time with them, they would always talk about their house in Mérida and the way they moved through it.

I can hear James still, the things that he would say. The last time I saw him, he told me to lean in for advice. I was thinking it was going to be profound. I wondered, "He's done it all—what pearls are going to be bestowed upon me?"

James said, "There's two things you need to know about life."

I was fully tuned in, waiting. *This is going to be it!*

"Stretch and save," he said.

I've never forgotten it, the realness of it and how grounded it was.

I'm always amazed by the ripple effect James and Alexandra had on everyone around them. To know them was to love them. If you met them for twenty minutes or if you knew them for ten years, it made an impact on your life.

. . .

The first time the three kids saw the property that would become this gorgeous home, Dagmar and Cosmas told me, it was a mess, a ruin. A group of young kids had been squatting there, and there was graffiti all over the walls. The front part of the house was the only part that was intact. The rest of the building, which they would later turn into the garden, was crowded with rubble and trash, overgrown weeds and jungle.

It's incredible to imagine it in this condition because every room in the house now is so decadent, every detail considered. Everywhere you look, your eye falls upon some curious object, or a wonderful work of art, or a spectacular architectural detail.

Back then, when they walked in, all they saw were rats and darkness.

Cosmas said, "This place is horrible."

This was when Dagmar was eleven, Cosmas was thirteen, and Degenhart was fifteen. They thought their parents had lost their minds. Coming from a beautiful hacienda in the middle of the countryside in Oaxaca, the children found this place in Mérida, the capital city of Yucatán, to be so chaotic, so different than what they were used to! But their parents had so much enthusiasm.

"You have to have vision," Alexandra told them. "Just be patient."

The house in Mérida was never meant to be a full-time home, just a temporary place to store everything from Oaxaca for a few years while they built a hacienda in the Yucatán jungle. During the winter months, they were in Mérida, but the hacienda in Yucatán was put

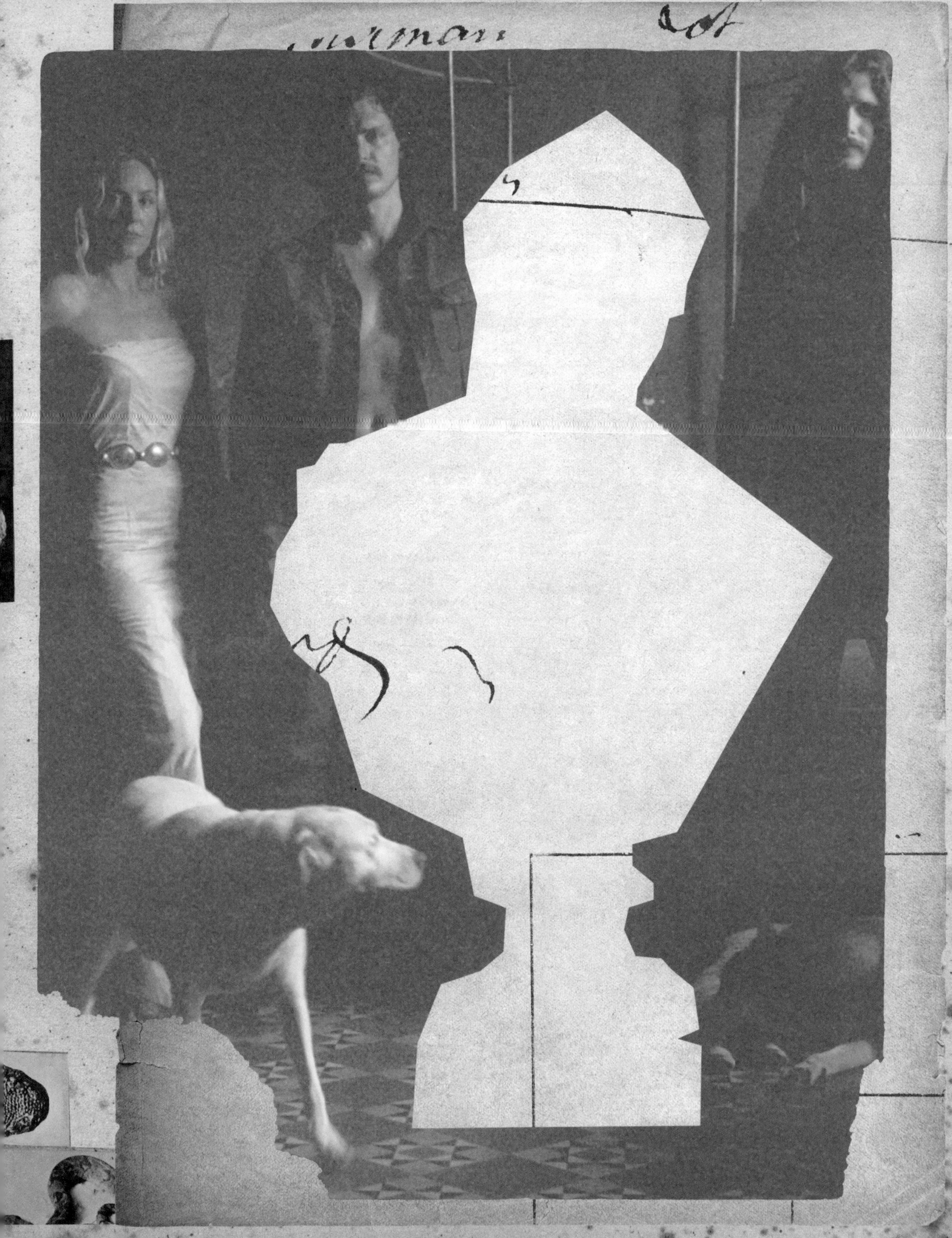

on hold once they realized how beautiful the house in Mérida was going to be. It took ten years for the house to become fully livable.

While the kids were in boarding school, Alexandra and James worked on the house in Mérida. As time went by, and they started really moving into the space and creating all its intricate designs, it became an even more important place for them. Mérida became a retreat from the world, where they could just work on their art. James found his art studio, where he worked with Lucio, the dog, whom he brought with him every day. Alexandra ran their press, Carpe Diem Books. There were also two cats, Mizti and Shatzi; James always joked that they weren't actually cats, but decorations, because you couldn't touch them. (If you tried, they would just run away!)

The couple developed a real routine in Mérida. They were very comfortable, and people always wanted to come and visit them and see their miraculous maze of a house.

Once they found this place, the space kept them. It was enough for them, an accidental paradise.

I looked through the door

As I walk through the house, it feels like such an accurate representation of Alexandra and James. They didn't use an architect or a designer to create it—the house was all their own ideas. They made it exactly how they wanted it. Dagmar enjoys the fact that half of the house didn't initially exist, but it looks completely original. She sees it as if her parents are saying, "We made this house look like it's been here since the very beginning, but we did it all ourselves."

• • •

and thought I saw James

James and Alexandra always told their children that home is where the heart is; wherever they were as a family, that's where home was. It was their habit, when it got too hot, in May, to spend six months in Europe, where they had close friends. During the winter months, they would live in Mérida.

The kids have absorbed their parents' habit of moving around all the time. They have lives that are layered, and they have the magical ability to be comfortable wherever they go.

I asked Dagmar and Cosmas what their idea of home was, and they referenced their home in Oaxaca, the one they grew up in. The home in Mérida was really James and Alexandra's, but every Christmas, the kids came home from boarding school to Mérida for a few weeks. What they remember from that time are the rituals. Every evening around 6:30, they would all gather.

"Mommy would say, 'Tea,'" Dagmar said. "And we'd all have to go and have tea in the kitchen."

That house calls for these ingrained routines to be repeated. They can't help but have tea, enjoy a drink outside, and have a cigarette before dinner, the way they all

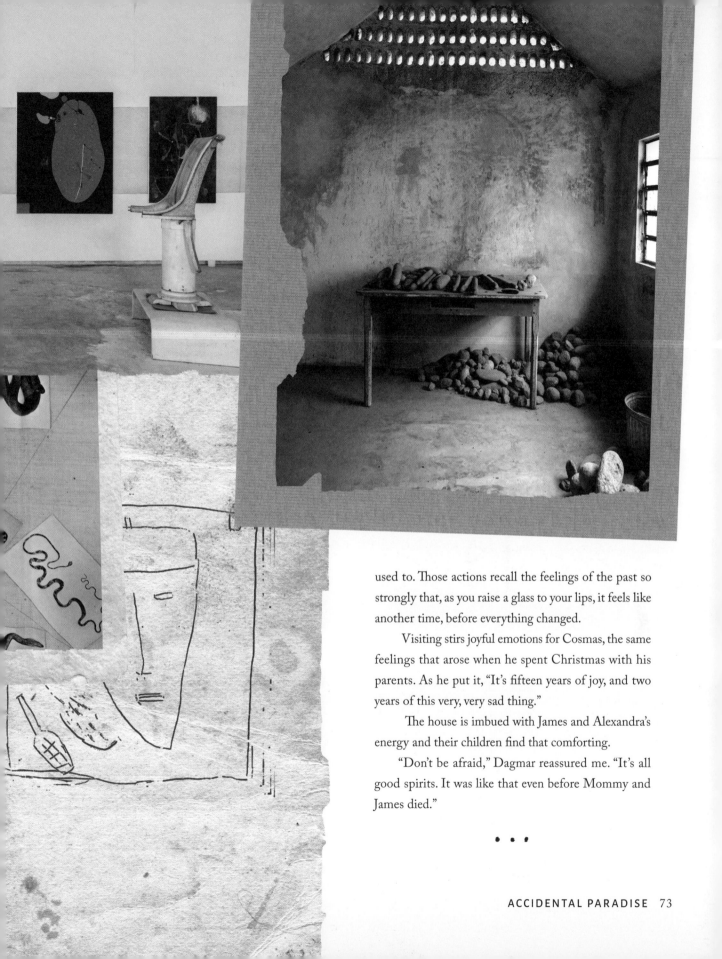

used to. Those actions recall the feelings of the past so strongly that, as you raise a glass to your lips, it feels like another time, before everything changed.

Visiting stirs joyful emotions for Cosmas, the same feelings that arose when he spent Christmas with his parents. As he put it, "It's fifteen years of joy, and two years of this very, very sad thing."

The house is imbued with James and Alexandra's energy and their children find that comforting.

"Don't be afraid," Dagmar reassured me. "It's all good spirits. It was like that even before Mommy and James died."

. . .

None of the children want to live in Mérida as they have busy lives elsewhere, but the house has a rhythm they still participate in. To Dagmar, coming to the house doesn't feel like coming home; it's more like a very special space that needs to be preserved as well as possible. What she's learned is that being a visitor to this home is a very different experience than maintaining it. It's a complicated structure. Their parents knew the intricacies of upkeep, and so does Jenny, who's been working in the house for 15 years. But Dagmar and Cosmas never had that conversation with their parents, and they are learning as they go.

Now that Dagmar, Cosmas, and Degenhart inhabit their parents' life in this house at times, they have realized why their parents were always working on this house, nonstop: because it's an endless battle. There's always something that needs to be taken care of.

"When people die," Dagmar said, "and then you're left with something beautiful, it's really up to you to decide what you want to do with it. It's not up to them anymore. It's just a continuation."

The voice in the back of their heads is James's voice, saying, "Get rid of the house if you want to. It doesn't matter. This is not your house. You don't have to take care of it if you don't want to. You don't have to do any of this stuff."

For now, they are committing themselves to the task.

It's so beautiful to hear that their preservation of the house isn't because of a sense of being caught up in something inescapable; it's a decision they have made willingly. They do it because they want to honor their parents' legacy.

Before James and Alexandra passed away, they bought a printing shop in Athens. Now that shop is a canvas for Dagmar and Cosmas to figure out the next family adventure.

What a gift their parents gave them—they gave themselves to their children, through their space.

It's just a

continuation...

CHAPTER FOUR

Treehouse In the City

BROOKE AND MICHAEL

In the way they move through the city, the way they walk down the street, Michael and Brooke are the quintessential New Yorkers. They're just part of the vibration of the West Village. I love going to Café Cluny and seeing Michael's image on the wall; the two of them are so polished, so chic, so elegant. He's a writer and an old-school magazine editor. She's an entrepreneur and fashion executive. I've always felt that people who don't know them well would be shocked to see not only how goofy they are, but also how vulnerable they are, and how warm—which is why I needed them to be a part of this book.

These two dear friends of mine are so thoughtful with the way they inhabit the world, down to the people, objects, and memories that they bring into the home, down to the way they display things: silver boxes, objects from their travels and numerous other unique and personal treasures. They've even framed pictures our children have drawn for them. They have two little woven figurines that they will leave in various places around the house to make each other smile, which I always have thought is so beautiful.

Brooke—Nate and I affectionately call her Brookie—has such a pride in the ownership of her home. Everything that she does in her home, whether it's entertaining, sweeping the floors, or cleaning the kitchen—she always talks about it with such joy. It makes such an impression on me.

Their relationship with this home is a love story that begins with a mistake and ends in serendipity. When I asked, Brooke and Michael were quick to say that the house chose them, and that they feel like they were meant for this space.

Their house has Brooke's soul in it, Michael told me. It's filled with light, serenity, calmness. Brooke's spirit sets the tone.

Before Michael and Brooke found each other, he had been in New York for twenty years, developing his writing career and running numerous magazines. He'd been renting for all of that time, a consummate New Yorker that way. He was of the city, but he didn't really have any roots in the city. A part of him had never wanted to buy anything until he had found that person that he could build something with. At some point, he stopped thinking that was ever going to happen to him.

Michael grew up in Chicago. He moved to New York City as a young man and lived in a room in a boarding house run by Quakers. It had a shared bathroom down the hall, where he had to wait in line to take a shower every morning. He paid $600 a month for that room, until he saved up a little money. Then, as he says, he came to the Village and never left.

The Village back then wasn't yet a neighborhood that people wanted to live in, but Michael was taken by the light and the river. The area had always loomed in his mind because it was so beautiful, and so he found himself a studio apartment. Over the years, he saved a little more, ("Like a squirrel," he says), and some years later, he got himself a one-bedroom apartment in the same building.

He was in his 40s, living in his little one-bedroom apartment, happy because it was in the perfect neighborhood, on the perfect street. He could lay in bed at night, and—even in this small room—he could see himself in this room, in this building, in this neighborhood, in this city that's at the center of the world. That was so heart-tingling to him. But he never referred to his place as a home. It was just his apartment. He was still hoping to find someone who he could build a home with.

Then he met Brooke, a woman who really cared about home on all levels. When I asked Brooke what home means to her, she told me about growing up in Naperville, Illinois, with a father who had excellent taste. Her childhood home was completely different than all of her friends'—modern, with great furniture. She also has a love of design and a desire to be surrounded by beautiful things, like her father, and her connection to home is about stability as much as beauty. What she really wants is a safe haven, a nest to come home to.

In her words, "You come home every day."

• • •

Brooke and Michael looked for the right apartment for what felt like a very long time. They knew they wanted to stay in the Village, so they had a very small radius. Things would come up, they would go look at them, and Brooke would fall in love, but Michael was more reticent. They found a couple of places they both liked, but all of them fell through, a series of huge disappointments.

Then came the spring of 2012, when a building on West 11th Street had an open house. Brooke and Michael walked into an apartment full of people and found a space by the window. They were in there for barely fifteen minutes, and what they remembered most when they left was the view when they looked out the windows, all the trees in bloom. It was such a different perspective from their current apartment, which was high and had a view of the cityscape.

I spent my whole life hoping to find you.

Their reaction was "Oh my God. We can never live here."

They were so anxious about their error. Their offer had been accepted, they had paid a deposit, and they wanted out. Michael thought that they should back out and lose their deposit, but Brooke wanted to figure it out.

Until they did, she said, they could just keep living in their one-bedroom rental. Michael started to use the new space as a writing and painting studio on the weekends, and he was happy to be working there, so it was a good temporary solution. After a couple of years, they thought, they would let the place go.

One day, Michael was writing in his studio when there was a little whoosh under the front door as an envelope slid through. The letter inside was from their next-door neighbor, who had noticed that they had never moved in. She wanted to buy the space. They agreed immediately. But after some weeks of back-and-forth talks, their neighbor realized that it was too much for her to combine the two apartments as she had originally planned—to which Brooke said, "Well, if you don't want to do that, can we buy yours?"

They talked about it on the way home—that view!—and decided to just put an offer in at the recommendation of their broker, knowing they probably wouldn't get it, but considering it a good exercise.

Two days later their offer was accepted.

They asked to come back and see the apartment again. This time, emptied of people, it was clear to them that they had made a huge mistake. It was much smaller than they remembered, and the layout—basically one room and a bedroom—wouldn't actually suit their needs at all.

I will
love
You Forever,
Brother
Mike

It's a space trust

Keeps us forever 21

You came home everyday

Before their neighbor introduced the idea, the concept of expansion wasn't on Brooke and Michael's radar. They were just so focused on the problem, which was that the apartment was too small for them to live there together. The whoosh of the letter under the door was a fairy-tale moment. It became a contract, which became a renovation, which became a home.

• • •

Now Brooke and Michael live in their dream home. They walk down 11th Street every day and think, "I can't believe we live on this street," because to them, it's one of the most beautiful streets in the city. Brooke's joy is sitting in the back of the apartment, looking out at magnolia and bamboo trees and seeing the woodpeckers. This home is their little treehouse in the city.

I asked them who they are in this home.

"Happy," said Michael.

"Very happy," agrees Brooke.

They are living the dream, but the dream is not just a three-bedroom, two-bath in Greenwich Village. Michael's dream was to build a home for the woman who loved him and saved him, and make it their safe, beautiful nest. He always dreamed of a home that would be a calm, safe port to pull into after a day on the stormy seas, and now he has one.

What Brooke gave him in this experience was the courage to leap. As much as he wanted to, he was so nervous. Brooke was the one who knew they should buy something, and to Michael, her plan for this home reflected one of her many great qualities. She's the one who said, "Trust this moment, and trust this. Trust us, and let's do this."

. . .

When Brooke and Michael combined two apartments into one home, they had the chance to create something that would be right for them. They were very deliberate about how they built it, very thoughtful and considerate. They thought, "What is this home? And what layers do we want to put into it?" Everything that is there, they labored over. They put so much thought and consideration into it that they love everything about their home: custom white-oak floors, vintage hardware throughout, marble fireplaces from the seventeenth and eighteenth centuries.

But not all the layers are on view. They burned sage in all the corners before they moved in; Michael had never done that before, and Brooke insisted they do it before they closed up the walls. There are a lot of hidden things behind the walls, too. They carved their initials into the cement. They added hearts and messages of love on the beams. They literally put their love in the bones of the building to make it go in deep.

"It isn't just what you see on the surface," Michael said to me. "It's what's in the beams and bones of a building."

If you ask Brooke, she will tell you that she feels like this house chose them, like they were meant for this space. The fact that they did it together brings them so much joy and happiness. It's the space that has allowed them to feel safe through losing jobs and going through tough times. It's a sanctuary, serene, with light and art and nature and beauty. They are constantly laughing together; this home makes them feel like they'll be 21 forever.

There's just so much love and joy in their house. It doesn't surprise me that they've etched hearts into beams, because they constantly show acts of love to each other. The way they live in their space is another act of love.

...the day of my life —
...my wife and
...you forever.

Nate

Merry
Christmas!
        Love,
        Mike

Sparkly
Shiny
Star.

Thank you for
Loving me.

I will love you
Forever.

I love you,
little click

Happy

Very Happy

Michaels dream was to build a home

For the woman who saved him and make it their safe beautiful nest

Roots and Vines

CORAL, DAVID, AND DENEEN

To cross the bridge that leads to the Brown Estate in Napa Valley is to enter a special place with its own kind of stillness. The moment you enter the property, there is an adventurous kind of energy that you feel, like you're going into a magical world. When you walk on the grounds, you can feel how special it is in the way the air moves through it. The property is surrounded by mountains, cradled in its own little valley, and the valley channels the prevailing breeze. On the front porch of the house, a beautiful breeze comes upon you. If you're in one of the upstairs bedrooms and you open the window, the breeze just comes right through, and blows through the house.

The 1885 house is old for the area, and unique because of its setting. In the horse-and-buggy days, a house built close to the road was desirable. But this home is set way back, so far back that you originally had to cross a bridge in order to arrive.

The story that Coral and David told me begins with their parents, Dr. Bassett and Mrs. Marcela Brown, who were looking for a second home in the 1970s. They were searching for a space that would give them three things: a place where they could commune with nature with their three kids every day; a place where they could farm and live off the land and be self-sufficient; and a place where they could all work together as a family.

It took ten years before they laid eyes on the ranch where they would plant their fields of grapes, the land that would eventually become the fabulous and esteemed Napa winery that Coral, David, and their sister, Deneen, launched in 1996 and run today. It is the first black-owned estate winery in the Napa Valley, and the wines they make are vibrant and heralded. The story of this place is interesting and complicated and beautiful, a family story that has stuck with Nate and I since we first heard it. I'm so inspired by what they have been through and what they've created and forged together. Even now, with all they have already created, they are continually in the process of imagining.

Before the siblings had ever seen it, their mom and dad had already begun a love affair with this place. When Marcela and Bassett discovered the house, it was abandoned, overgrown, untouched since the 1930s—a project. Part of that struck a chord with these people who had been on a search to find a property for a decade.

Marcela believed that if a property is really for you, you know in the first five minutes. That was the experience she had when she set foot on this property in Napa in 1980. When she arrived, right before she crossed the bridge, she felt an aura of peace and tranquility, and a calm to her being. She and Bassett were in love with the purity of the place.

The kids were less enthralled when they were first introduced to the property. It was a "ruin," David told me. What their parents had described as a magical place—so much so that they were expecting an actual fairy-tale castle—was anything but. "It was uninhabitable," Coral said. "There were 250,000 bats living in there."

Not that they were unaccustomed to their parents' sense of adventure. Three years before they found this space, the family had moved to Jamaica, a shift in lifestyle that Coral described as "really a shock." Still, they found the state of the rundown Napa house to be jarring.

They slept those first nights with bats flying around their heads.

"To this day," said David, "if you leave a window open at night, the bats will come in."

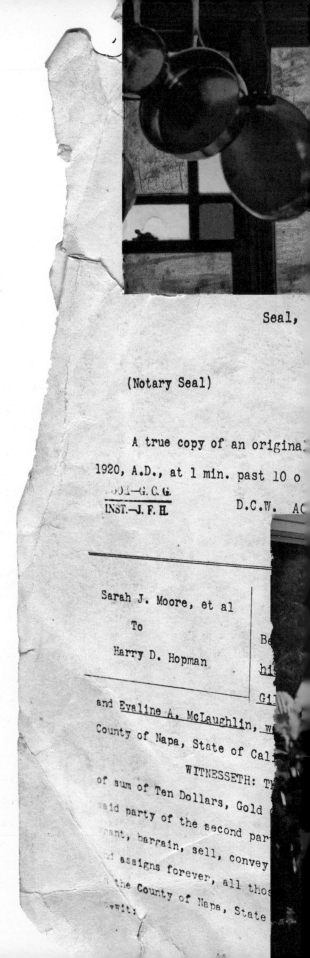

y and year in this certifi   wr1

S. Barnum

y Public in and for said County of

da, State of California

ded at the request of Napa County Abstract Co.

1.M.

.10

Recc

A.D.

ncy

and

, of

derat

d by

e pre

Our Mom and Dad
loved this place so much
it really
was their
love affair
with the place

The house was so wild that David still refuses to go camping, even when his friends make fun of him for it.

"We camped for ten years," he will say. "I don't like to go camping."

Over time, what this family was able to create was an incredible fusion between the past and the present. From the outside, the house was in shambles, but within, they found a roll top desk that had artifacts from the history of the property, like the original deed stating that the property was sold for ten dollars' worth of gold coins in the 1920s.

All of the architectural detail had been stripped from the house. Most people would have just knocked the building down, but Marcela and Bassett wanted to restore it. Every Saturday and Sunday, they would wake the kids to work in the garden of their house in Pasadena. They knew the work would be multiplied when they were up in Napa—and it was, exponentially.

The kids were dragged up there for every summer, every holiday, always working and learning, never relaxing. Once they bought the ranch in 1980, David said, they never took another vacation.

"That was it," Coral said.

"That was it," her brother agreed.

• • •

1990

For a long time, the property was a work in progress. As the kids remember it, the entire front of the property was like a grove of old walnut trees. It was just wild; you could hardly see the house through the forest of cotoneasters. Behind the thicket, the house had a big lawn with two magnificent trees, a walnut tree and a California bay laurel. They needed to remove one of the trees to make space or the driveway, but it wasn't an easy decision. Basset hated the idea of taking either down. They went over and over it in their heads. Finally, they decided to take the walnut down and keep the California bay laurel, which still stands today.

Throughout their landscaping and renovation processes, the family wanted to honor the ancient history of this land while making it their own. The house had been abandoned since the 1930s, and had become so run down, that it took years to painstakingly restore it.

The children remember fondly how rustic the kitchen was at the beginning, complete with a wood burning stove. Cooking became a big part of their lives because once you were on the ranch, there was no easy way to go to a shop to pick up a snack. If they wanted a meal, it required thoughtful preparation and execution, which typically began with chopping wood and building a fire in the original wood-burning stove.

A lot of Coral's memories of the early days in that house have to do with the cooking. The family would come up every Thanksgiving and cook dinner on the old, antique stove. Marcela cared deeply about the food her family consumed and was particular about health and nutrition. She was a talented cook and made all of her meals from scratch. All that focus on food gave the children a love and appreciation for flavor, which plays into the wines they make on the property today.

David remembers all five of them coming up to work on the house one Thanksgiving. There was no furniture inside yet—no beds, nothing. They all slept on the floor in the living room. The house smelled like paint because they were putting on the primer coat. David woke up in the middle of the night and saw the fire going while everyone was sleeping. That's what he pictures when he looks at the house.

would keep the original wooden post because that was where they would gather in the little entry hall for family meetings to brainstorm, to dream, to be disciplined. Those moments linger in that space, and the post remains, a silent witness to it all.

• • •

It wasn't easy to restore this home, and through the years, there were times when holding onto the ranch was a struggle. Coral remembered one moment in particular when they were living in Pasadena. Her dad was running his medical practice, and it would have been so much easier to sell the ranch and focus on life in the city. But Bassett was resolute. The ranch was his passion. If he sold that ranch, he told Marcela, he would have no reason to work anymore. And Marcela said, "Okay." Against all odds they kept it and grew it into something incredible.

There is a post at the base of the staircase in the entry hall that holds a lot of memories for Deneen. The stairs were small and the original wooden banister was too short and too shaky. Coral replaced it with a wrought-iron banister that was sturdier. Deneen was clear that, even when they replaced the banister, they

It was a passion that he shared with his children, who helped to paint the house, including the intricate balustrades. Coral and Deneen went to college at UC Berkeley, where there was an architectural salvage store, and their dad would give them assignments to track down items that were needed at the ranch: "Find 75 brass butt hinges with carvings on them." They would get to looking until they found them. These experiences taught them to love this work. It taught them the concept of restoration.

It gave us all a sense of autonomy,

It wasn't until the kids were older that they truly realized what they had in the ranch: their own world, a space to create whatever they wanted, with nobody in charge of them.

"For me," said David, "having all of the privacy and the space to grow up and make mistakes without having the whole world see your mistakes was really critical for my development."

As Coral put it, "It gave us all a sense of autonomy, a sense of freedom, a sense of control over our life and our future."

I asked what their parents' relationship with the ranch was, over time.

Coral had a ready answer: "It really was their love affair with the place."

• • •

In 1996, the three siblings launched the Brown Estate label when they harvested the grapes that would become their first bottles of Brown Zin. Stewardship of the land is one of their pillars, which is why the wines they produce are California-certified organic. There are seven natural springs on the property that combine to form the headwaters of the Napa River, the ranch is part of the original pass that settlers used to get from Sacramento and San Francisco to the Napa Valley in the mid-nineteenth century. The property is in an area that is rich in history, going back to the indigenous people who settled here ten thousand years ago. The Brown siblings can feel the history, the legacy, and the souls of the people who were here before.

a sense of freedom, a sense of control over our life and future

Coral and David told me that they are intimately familiar with every corner of this property, in part because their parents would bring them on long hikes. They dreaded going on those hikes as children, but they now admit it helped them get to know their land, and that some of the spots they discovered together are still their favorite places here.

"This place has been a refuge for every single member of our family," said David. "There are certain aspects to the property that make you feel very private and secure, in your own world."

David loves a place at the top of the hill, where you can look out and see the vista. That's his happy place. Coral's pick is on the west side of the property on the hillside, on the way to David's favorite spot, a place with magnificent 300-year-old oak trees. It has a filtered view, she explained, and it feels cradled and connected.

After Bassett's death, in 2019 the children felt a strong responsibility to the ranch.

"Now that we've lost dad, it's like an existential feeling that's come into play that wasn't there before," said Coral. "We can feel his presence—channel his spirit and his energy. And it's here. It is here."

• • •

Today, David lives in another house with his own family, yet the ranch will always feel like his home. For Coral, the property represents their collective heart.

In 2009, the siblings redesigned the front of the house. The designer warned them not to be too attached to the bay laurel that Basset and Marcela had loved so much, because they weren't going to design around a tree.

In the end the tree lined up perfectly with the front door, a great relief, because they wanted to hold on to the tree that their parents wouldn't part with. It is an important part of their landscape. It's a medicinal bay, Coral explained to me, the leaves of which are used in Jamaica to make bay rum. She remembers having dengue fever as a child and lying on her bed being doused in the stuff. Even now, she said, the essence of California bay laurel is noted in the tasting notes for their wines.

When she breaks up the leaves on the bay laurel tree that is in front of the house, she can smell that bay rum, and the scent carries her back to another time.

"Our mom and dad loved this place so much," said Coral. "It was the culmination of their hopes, their dreams, and their aspirations."

It really was their love affair with the place

CHAPTER SIX

a Farm in the Countryside

ANDRE

Years ago, at a storied and terrible dinner with a fake princess who left without telling anyone and never paid, I met Andre. He was so sweet to me and so inclusive, so warm. I've loved him since the first moment we met, and through all the years since.

Andre is an art dealer who is the most mischievous person I know. He intrigues me, because he lives so beautifully, and he is so ceremonial with the way he moves through the world. He would host late dinner parties, and he knew everybody, and his place was the spot that people went to. He was always a quintessential New Yorker to me.

So it was a shock when, seemingly out of nowhere, he picked up and moved to the Portuguese countryside, an hour and a half by car from Lisbon. When he didn't soon come back, a shockwave went through all of our friends. None of us were expecting this gentleman art dealer to become a countryside farmer. Neither was he! But things changed in his life, and an opportunity arose—and when he took it, he couldn't have guessed where it would lead.

• • •

116

Andre was raised in Portugal with his five brothers and his sister on a farm that his father purchased out of love. It is a place that no longer exists because it was destroyed by a fire in 2000; Andre recalls it with such fondness.

Nearly a decade later, Andre found himself looking for a farm of his own. He had a vision of something that was deep in the countryside, something isolated and spectacular. He had no particular purpose in mind—he wasn't ready to actually move to a farm, not yet. At the time, he was living in New York with no thought of leaving. He just wanted to have a house and some land in Portugal.

Andre was sitting at his father's bedside in the hospital when he first saw a picture of a rural estate that had come up for sale. His father was very ill, and Andre had

been with him all day. They looked at the pictures together: a simple yellow and white house that looked completely abandoned, in a beautiful summertime setting.

The two men were not close, but this was something they connected over. The dream of a farm was something both of them understood. Andre's father liked the property and insisted that his son go see it.

It was a Thursday when they looked at those images. Andre agreed to go see the place, but he didn't go right away. He spent all of that day and that night with his father. On Friday, Andre's dad passed away. With his five brothers away, it fell upon Andre to call family and friends to tell them that the patriarch of their family had passed away, and to manage the details for the funeral, which was held on Saturday.

On Sunday, he drove out to see the house. It was a long drive, and he was grateful for the distance because it was a moment for him to begin to process the emotions that were rising up after his father's passing.

It only took a glimpse of the main house to make him fall in love with the possibilities. He saw immediately how it would be to live here in the warm weather, with all of the windows open, and the wind blowing, the smell of blooming orange trees wafting through. As a lover of antiquities and archeology, especially from the Roman period, he had longed for a reason to buy marble sculptures. Looking at the house, he envisioned it done in white, with Roman sculptures here and there, with very old pieces of furniture mixing with pieces from the Sixties and Seventies.

Along with the main house, there were several smaller houses, but it was the land that drew him in right away. This farm had only 32 hectares, making it smaller than other places he'd seen, and it was more convenient to the city than the properties that were located in very agricultural areas. If he bought this place, he would have less land to manage and would still be able to keep dealing art.

Clearly in love, he bought the property in June and closed in July. Four weeks later, history repeated itself, and there was a huge fire, just as there had been on his father's farm. In this case, it was an electrical fire that had started in another place, crawled down the hill, and raged across the land.

It was the first fire anyone in the area could remember in a hundred years, Andre told me, recounting the sadness of the experience.

He pointed to a single perfect olive tree in the distance that has sprung from a singed disfigured trunk and said, "The baby rising from the ashes of its burnt mother."

After the fire, Andre's brother flew a drone over the farm, taking a series of photographs. The fire destroyed—and it also revealed. They discovered two fountains that had previously been completely covered by vegetation, and for the first time, they could see the lines of the irrigation system, a system of tiled channels that carry the water through the property—glimmers among the ruination. The channels reminded Andre of stone channels that had been a part of his family's farm, he told me.

Despite these discoveries, it was so soon after the purchase of the farm, so soon after the loss of his father, that he had no energy for rebuilding. Andre felt stalled and stuck, and for a year, he did nothing with the farm. As the months went by, he felt he should create a plan for the house. Was he going to sell it? Was he going to rebuild and replant? He didn't know. But he did know that he was going to Portugal for his friend Giancarlo's birthday party and for the Easter holidays.

He started at Giancarlo's party in Lisbon, where he stayed for two days. Since he had forgotten his driver's license back home in New York, he took an Uber from Lisbon to the farm, where he found himself in the countryside with no license and no driver, he told me.

He had packed a suitcase with enough clothes for a week. But a week came and went, and he did not leave.

"I came," said my friend, "and I stayed."

There was a lot for him to do, once he started taking stock. There were the main house and various smaller buildings to attend to, and there was the land. The process of beginning to work on the farm made him feel happy again, connected. He felt like he had gone back in time, to that space of being a child and wishing for his own farm and his own animals to care for. Working on his land in this way felt uncomplicated and honest.

Andre's revelation was that he was no longer happy in New York. He had been accumulating emotional and mental weight, and he had lost some of the old excitement he had about art. He longed to feel it again. What he needed was to reconnect with inspiration and passion, and he found that in his work on the farm and in restoring the main house.

I asked how his father would feel if he saw him in this place.

"I think he would be concerned about cost," he laughed, and told me that his father would have been proud to see that he didn't leave his art business behind when he made this big change. Andre thinks his father would have loved to see him here and would have given him fantastic advice.

Their family farm had been his father's baby, always his father's dream. This farm is Andre's dream.

• • •

Going to Andre's home for the first time was unnerving; it is as rural as rural can get, an hour and a half outside the city. But walking the property, I felt right away what he loved about it: it was so grounding, and it felt so good, so familiar. My grandmother is Portuguese and my mother has always talked about wanting to move there. Portugal is a place that has been on my mind, but I was not expecting to feel a sense of calm and quiet in the way that I did.

On our first night there, Andre said, "We're going to have dinner tonight, and it will be at ten o'clock." This sounded very late to me, but I was still awake at 10:30 p.m. when we started, and we were still playing Monopoly, many bottles of white wine later, at 3:00 a.m. The life here is just a different life. The days are longer. The evenings are closer and more intimate. Everything just feels more connected.

Visiting Andre in Portugal made me feel how the spaces we choose can change us. The effects on my friend are obvious; he was always so much fun and so dynamic, and he still is all of those things, but now he is leading with warmth and tenderness. Perhaps this shift stems from caring for the land and the animals, from taking care of this property and revitalizing it. Whatever the source, I found him to be so sweet and nurturing! It was a profound experience to see him this way.

I love seeing this softer, happier Andre. There is a kindness and peace in his smile. He shines with his purpose: to preserve and create life.

His next project is restoring the main house. At the moment, the whole main floor is open, waiting for him to be inspired. It's a big house, and only he lives there now, so there are still rooms he hasn't figured out. "I need to understand what I'm doing there," he said.

Until then, just the top floor is plenty of space for him. He only has two bedrooms, his and a spare. With plenty of smaller guest houses on the property, there's no need for more than one guest bedroom in the house.

For many years, this house was preserved, a time capsule kept the way it was. But when it was owned by a person that had no love for the house, a lot of important architectural features were destroyed.

I asked what he would want someone else to know if he were passing the house to them. He told me that he would want them to understand that this place is more than a real estate investment, that it is a property that should be preserved. He is committed to the integrity of the house, going so far as to preserve things that now-adays don't make much sense, like the irrigation system he and his brother uncovered after the fire. There are hundreds of meters of these channels for the water, and they are all inlaid with tiles. Andre has already restored most of them, but there is more work to do.

I came

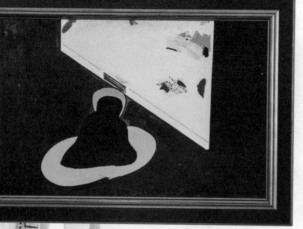

and

I Stayed

• • •

Andre's life here is a great contrast to his city life. One thing that he misses—laughing as he said this—is having a good gym to go to. He also misses his dinner parties and late nights enjoying his friends. Still, he does not want to go back. Here, he is in touch with nature, with the animals, with the land. Here, his schedule changes with the seasons. He wakes late, around nine, has his breakfast, and then goes outdoors to see what's going on. He's always renovating, organizing construction, restoring walls. Every morning he does his walk, then comes back to the office and works.

In the spring, he does a lot of work by himself outdoors, changing the plants to new pots, and putting new soil in. "You need to trim the bushes, prune the trees, and all that," he told me. "I like to do it by myself because I know how I want them to grow, so it's a job that is done by me."

He's been working on the property for five years now, and everything he does, he does with such pride. I get the sense that, despite his attention to detail, his love for this place isn't just about the home or this particular farm, but about the life he has there. It's the idea of the farm and what it connects him to in practice and in spirit. He has this big connection to the rural life; he knows what it is and he loves it: a simpler way of being, just like he wished for as a child—just like his father must have wished for with his own dream of a farm.

Living like this brings him home.

CHAPTER SEVEN

The Memory Palace

BIANCA AND GIBERTO

The first memory that Giberto, who is called Gibi by his friends, recalls is from when he was a child of five or six. It was summertime, and he was in his bedroom in his family's Venetian palazzo on the Grand Canal. It was nighttime, and the windows were open, because it was very, very, very hot. Telling me about it, he remembered that there was a gondola passing by, and a man singing "Santa Lucia."

The gondola, the sensation of that period—"It still comes to me sometimes, from now to then," he said.

Every room in the palace has its own stories, every room holds a piece of his childhood and his family's history. His father's studio on the second floor is now the library of the hotel Aman Venice, to whom he has leased the property for the next hundred years in a bid to save it. When Gibi passes through, he has that feeling of being a child, running around while his father sits at the table.

He knows the place so well, inside and out. He knows how the colors change with the seasons. June and September have the most beautiful light in the city, he told me.

The gleam of that early summer and early autumn light are sights he has experienced all his life. Year by year, they return, and always the same.

• • •

Life in the palazzo has been good to Gibi, the Count of Venice, and his wife, Bianca, the former princess of Savoy. But some moments along the way have had their challenges.

Gibi was born in this palazzo, a home that has been in his family for generations and is one of the largest on the Grand Canal of Venice. He inherited this place, complete with its gardens, frescoes, and otherworldly views of the canal, when he was eighteen years old.

Gibi's family's relationship with this house began with a gift. The palazzo itself had been commissioned in the sixteenth century and, in the eighteenth century, passed into the hands of the Tiepolo family, who left their signature in the form of the elaborately painted frescoes that adorn numerous walls throughout the home. In the nineteenth century, when a wealthy count wanted to give his bride something special, he chose this palace, through which his name still echoes: Palazzo Papadopoli. The count was Gibi's ancestor, who also purchased the adjacent palazzo solely so that he could knock it down and make space for gardens and another wing.

The count and his wife had two daughters, one of whom was Gibi's grandmother. She inherited the house upon her father's death and lived there with her family. Gibi's father grew up there in the 1920s, and Gibi was born there.

When his father was a boy, he told me, the family still inhabited the entire palace. There were six people in the family, and eighty people working for them. "Can

you believe it?" he exclaimed. "Eight zero!" By the time Gibi was born, the palazzo had been largely rented out to cover the rising costs; young Gibi and his family inhabited an apartment.

It has been four decades since Gibi and Bianca moved in, and they have lived in this architectural masterpiece ever since, raising their children here, working and struggling to pay the bills on this magnificent property. During tough times, Gibi told me, his ancestors had chosen to sell precious heirlooms, because they were never going to let the palazzo itself go. It was the same for Gibi. Even when upkeep became nearly impossible, he and Bianca held on.

He is proud of what he has accomplished through sweat and effort, doing whatever he could to stay in the palazzo.

• • •

Gibi hasn't always lived in this home. When he was eight, his family moved to the countryside because his father was very sick. His father was sixty-two years old, and Gibi remembers him as an old man with a pipe in his mouth, who would wake him for school in the mornings. He'd stick Gibi's head under the cold water of the tap for washing up, even though it was a freezing-cold December, while Gibi's sisters were given the luxury of warm water. As a World War II war hero, Gibi's father wanted his son to grow up like a soldier.

When Gibi's father died just a year later, the family moved to Rome. The years that followed were hard on them. Gibi's father had left the palazzo to him and his two sisters, and everybody they knew was saying, "Sell it, sell it, sell it." There was so much debt and they didn't have the money to pay it off.

"Never," said Gibi.

When Gibi turned eighteen and came of age, the palazzo became his responsibility. His mother had sold all the furniture that was inside, so the building was empty. He rented the palace out in order to be able to hold onto it; his only goal was to not have to sell. That was his miracle: to keep the house.

"It was a surrender, to sell it," he told me. "It's too easy to sell. All the big families in Venice have sold palazzos on palazzos, because they couldn't be bothered to fight for it. I've been fighting since I'm eighteen."

In 1988, Gibi married Bianca, a sophisticated princess from the French countryside. He was twenty-seven when they moved back into the palazzo, and Bianca was only twenty-two, young enough that, as she puts it, "You don't really know what you're doing and where you're going." She was coming from "tiny places" in Paris and in Milan, and suddenly found herself in this apartment in a palazzo, a "grown-up's house in Venice."

Venice was very different for her, interesting and strange and colorful. It was another era of Venice, she told me. At the time, there were fewer tourists and more Venetians, so that it was "much more of a normal city," as she put it.

Gibi and Bianca had their first child a few years later, and over the next decade had four more. They have lived there ever since, raising their children, managing the palazzo, trying to keep the lights on.

• • •

In 2007, a friend phoned Gibi saying that Adrian Zecha of the Aman hotel group wanted to meet him. Gibi said, "I don't want to do a hotel," but Adrian really wanted to see the palazzo. Most of the building was completely empty, because if Gibi ever wanted to rent out the whole, he'd be unable to do so if even a small part was already leased. As he said, it was complicated.

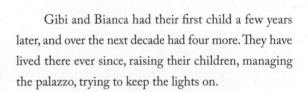

«Amor, ch'al cor gentil ratto
s'apprende, / prese costui della
bella persona / che mi fu tolta,
e 'l modo ancor m'offende.

Amor, ch'a nullo amato amar
perdona, / mi prese del costui
piacer sì forte / che, come vedi,
ancor non m'abbandona.

Amor condusse noi ad una
morte. / Caina attende chi a vita
ci spense», Queste parole
da lor ci fur porte.

He agreed to meet Adrian, who turned out to be the most charming man you'll ever meet in your life, according to Gibi. As they walked around the palazzo, it only took half an hour for them to become the best of friends. They toured all seven thousand meters, and when they sat down in the studio to talk, Gibi was surprised to find that Adrian remembered all of it, all of the rooms, where they were, which staircases led to them. Even Gibi, who had been born in the palazzo, grew up there, and was raising his children there, sometimes needed to make an effort to hold the complete picture of everything in his mind. Gibi was amazed by how quickly Adrian had absorbed the intricacies of his home.

"I want this place," Adrian told Gibi. "I've been looking for a place in Venice for fifteen years."

"Listen," Gibi responded. "I don't want to sell it."

Adrian smiled, a big smile, and said, "Gibi, you know what we do? You don't sell, we rent."

Gibi had a list of requirements. He knew that if the hotel didn't work out, he'd need to rent the rooms as apartments, so he required that the renovations include no more than forty rooms. He reminded Adrian that the building is a historical monument of national interest and would have

to be renovated carefully as such. And, most important, Gibi said, "I live here with my wife and my five children, and I really don't want to go away."

"We're very happy," Adrian told him. "Forty is more than enough. Maybe we'll do less. You live here with your children and your wife. My guests will be delighted to meet you."

Gibi agreed.

"Now it should work until I die," Gibi said to me. "I hope."

With the introduction of their shared vision for restoration, the building has been returned to its original glory, and Gibi's family occupies the top floor of the Palazzo Papadopoli.

During the pandemic, Venice, usually so busy with tourists and visitors, emptied out, and all five of Gibi and Bianca's children came to stay with them. The family spent their mornings in the garden in the sun, did their workouts in the ballroom, and ate out of the hotel kitchen and fridges so that the food that had already been stored there wouldn't go to waste. They played cards, took breaks for their various business meetings, and then gathered for lunch and dinner. It was a surreal and wonderful experience for them, living in a hotel with no guests, just family. Even when the hotel is full of guests, his family is still able to roam the grounds as they have for more than 150 years.

The way it has all turned out makes Gibi very happy. Bianca feels the same way.

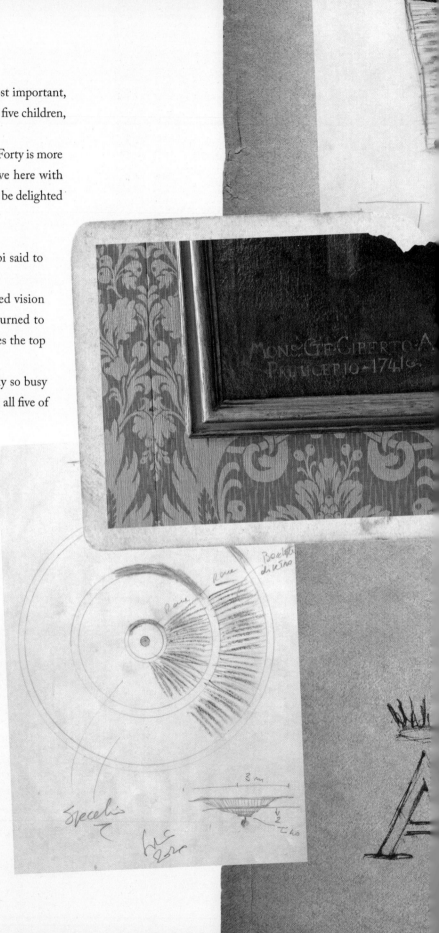

VETRO

2cm

INCISIONE

VERDE

VETRO

Deux
2.5.3.94.

8 cm Pasta K0?

20 cm

Alessa

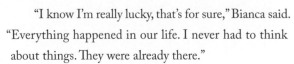

"I know I'm really lucky, that's for sure," Bianca said. "Everything happened in our life. I never had to think about things. They were already there."

"Because I was thinking of everything," her husband added, teasing.

I can't imagine either of them living anywhere but here. Bianca is part of the rhythm of life here. Gibi is an extension of that house. Their life on the very top floor of this massive palazzo is beautiful and simple, yet still incredibly sophisticated.

Anyone who sees Gibi walking through that space can just feel that he belongs to the palazzo, and that it belongs to him.

"Will you stay forever?" I asked.

Gibi nudged Bianca to answer, knowing she would have the right phrase in mind.

"Bella, I think it's wonderful," he said to her. "It was fantastic."

She offered me an Italian adage, which she then translated into English: "I'll only get out of here with my feet ahead."

It's the Tuscan version of "They'll have to carry me out."

They'll Have
to carry Me
Out

CHAPTER EIGHT

A House Like a Hug

TRACY AND BRIAN

Nothing about Tracy and Brian's house is what I might have expected them to have. I know them as people whose first direction of design is sleek, elegant, and structured, but here they are, in love with a space full of antiques. This 2000-square-foot, three-bedroom, single-story home in Montecito is not their main residence, but it is the home they feel most connected to. Once I was in there, it all made sense. That's why I needed to include them in this book, and why I asked them to talk with me about their love for this home.

"I would have never in a million years thought that this was a place that we would have lived in, style-wise," Tracy told me. The design is very much the way the previous owner styled it because Tracy and Brian love it so much. They hung some art but, for the most part, they left the furniture that was there. They didn't want to change the home; they wanted to feel embraced by it as it was.

"You could walk into the most beautiful, expensive house, and it just has no energy. It just doesn't have a vibe," Brian said. "This is a house that is tiny and simple, but it just has this warmth and holds you."

Their house has something special in it, and it very much reminds me of the warmth of the family that lives in it. In addition to Tracy and Brian are Miles and Justin, Brian's sons from a previous marriage, and Stella. We met when Nate and I designed a home for them in Los Angeles, and I was so taken with who they are as human beings, and how they interact as a family. They are an amazing bunch. What they value is the sense of belonging in that house, where everything is centered around connection. Every area is rooted in sitting together and coming together.

When you're there, you're a part of everything.

• • •

Brian's first encounter with this home began with a casual perusal of property listings. A real estate enthusiast, he was reading through listings as he always does, when he saw the ad in *Variety* and had a real wow moment. Tracy wanted to see it too. She thought it looked amazing and envisioned a quick drive to Montecito to see it. They could spend the night at San Ysidro Ranch, where they had gotten married. Brian was less eager about the idea of a road trip, but Tracy's enthusiasm carried them along.

They drove up the coast, Tracy remembered, and as soon as they pulled into the gates, there was a state of disbelief. "That field of purple flowers is to the left," she said, setting the scene for me. "We were just looking at each other like, 'Okay. This is kind of crazy. The house must just be awful.' Right?,' Cause it's so beautiful."

The next thing that came into view on top of a hill was the little house with the porch. Once inside, Brian found the house to be spectacularly charming. The way it was decorated felt peaceful and perfect.

It wasn't until they stepped off the porch and onto the back steps that they got a real sense of the property: there was a pool, and landscaped levels, and mountains, and a one-hundred-year-old barn with a barreled ceiling. They were blown away. Walking the property, they had the feeling that it went on and on.

The property is big and the house is small. As people who were accustomed to living in spacious homes—in that moment they were living in an 11,000-square-foot home—they were surprised by how taken they were with this little house. There hadn't been any photos showing how small the interior is, and they willingly admit that they might not have even made the drive in the first place if they'd known.

Once they were there, they succumbed to the charms of the place. This was the house they wanted. They put an offer on the place, went on vacation to Saint-Tropez, and closed within three weeks. I was on that trip to Saint-Tropez with them and I remember how thrilled they were, how excited, how sure. I couldn't wait to see it for myself.

When I walked in, I got it immediately.

. . .

Tracy and Brian intended this home to be a refuge for their family, an escape from their very busy professional and social lives. When they purchased it, the pandemic had not yet swept through and changed everything. It was before the death of George Floyd and the ensuing riots in Los Angeles. It amazes them still that this all happened pre-Covid, pre-knowing.

They had no idea that it would be an actual escape, or that they were about to spend the next two years there. Tracy is a Black woman and their three kids are Black. When Los Angeles exploded in protests, it became even more important for them to take the kids and go.

"We spent Election Night in that house," said Brian. "We had gone out of LA for a while because we were scared about the geopolitical issues. All the protests were happening in Beverly Hills, down the street from us. Every weekend there were these enormous protests leading up to the election. We were scared of what might happen."

At the house, they watched the news all day on Election Day. Tracy went to bed at eight o'clock that night, but Brian couldn't sleep at all. He lay on the couch in the living room all night, until dawn, and watched CNN.

When you're there you're a part of everything

In Los Angeles, the tensions were unrelenting. In Montecito, the family could choose when to watch the news and when to shut the TV off and get back into the peaceful rhythms of nature. When Tracy worried that Stella, their youngest, was absorbing their stressed, worried energy, she knew they had a place where they could disconnect from their fear—and connect with one another instead.

"We could watch it, turn off the TV, and then seek refuge in the home we were in and just focus on being a family, and loving each other," said Tracy.

When it comes to the house they love, everything they talk about is rooted in refuge, including its location. The air changes when the highway crosses over the mountains and reaches the Pacific.

"You see the ocean," Tracy explained, "and you really do feel like you're in a whole other place mentally and physically."

The house imbues them with the feeling that they can go there and just be. Their life at the house is super mellow. They lounge. They relax. They don't feel pressed to do anything or go anywhere.

"It's early morning..." Brian lays it out for me. "You open up the doors. You take your cup of coffee, you go out there. When it rains, a stream starts going under the porch."

There's something about the vibe up there that he connects to. He loves being in a place where he can wake up in the morning, go walk on the beach, and then take a hike in the country. It's a place where summer feels like summer, and in the winter, Stella can play in the snow.

Their dogs love it too. In LA, Brian said, they're "like house cats. Up there they get to run around and go crazy." The same goes for the people. "We just love it," he said.

If it were up to him, they would live in Montecito full time.

• • •

For both Tracy and Brian, home is about the people more than the place. When Tracy thinks of home, she thinks of Stella, Brian, Miles, and Justin. "It doesn't feel like home until everybody's with you," Tracy said. "All the people that you love."

Connection is so important to these two individuals, and the house is the epitome of that. The stuff in the house doesn't matter; it's the way they live in the space that helps them appreciate what it brings to them.

Growing up, Brian lived in the same house until he was fourteen, when he moved to California. Tracy grew up on military bases and her family moved every two years. On military bases, she told me, all of the homes are sort of the same. Her first real memory of home stems from the time her family lived in Japan, when she was seven. What she remembers is the cultural experience of being there. She thinks that it's easy for her to move around a lot now because she moved so many times in her youth—so falling in love with a place the way they have here, in Montecito, is a moment that she notices and appreciates.

It doesn't feel like home

until everybody's with you

It's fascinating to me that even without the personalization that comes with a new renovation, this whole place feels intrinsically like them. They thought about ripping up the dark floors and putting in new wood herringbone, and they considered making the beams real wood instead of just painted, and they discussed pushing the kitchen out to expand it. But they soon realized that if they did all that, the house would be fussy. It wouldn't be the same. None of that is necessary, because the house works for them as it is, with its feeling of comfort and coziness and ease. It's gorgeous, but simple.

They've learned a lot living here, and what they have come to see is that they need less space than they imagined. In their larger home, they're always all in separate rooms, and it's so easy to hide out in different places and never see each other. In Montecito, when they're there, they are really there. Stella's room is right across the hall from Brian and Tracy's, and she can run between them easily. They love how enveloped they feel.

There are so many moments in this house that hold them: the fireplace, which is always on, even if it's 90 degrees out; the screened-in porch, where the day at the house begins and ends. Even when the temperature drops, they still go out there for coffee in the morning or for an evening cocktail.

Long summer days are wonderful at the house, with the pool in the backyard, everything in full bloom, and the hummingbirds outside in the lavender field. They can hear the sound of the water rushing by. They can smell the summer air. The environment is an integral part of the experience of the house. When they are here, they feel so connected to nature, like they're part of the world around them.

I asked if they will ever leave it.

"I don't think we'll ever sell it," said Tracy.

"No, don't ever say never," Brian replied. "You just never know, right?"

She understood him immediately.

"You're right," she said to him, and she explained to me: "We've learned now that we can never answer a question when it comes to homes. You just don't know what your next home could be. You could walk into something magical a year from now, and wherever you are in your life, that might be where you need to be."

For now, though, this is where they belong. To them, it's been an incredible place; a special place; a happy, peaceful place.

"Like it was a hug," Tracy said. "A big old hug."

CHAPTER NINE

The Light on the Balcony

DORA AND NINO

For thirty-five years, Dora has been cooking in the same little kitchen in her light-filled apartment in the town of Giarre, on the east coast of Sicily. "Really, for fifty years," she corrects herself, because she and her husband Nino have been married for fifty years, and most of what is in this room came with them from their first home. "This is an old kitchen," she said—the only things she has replaced are the appliances.

When Dora talks about what she loves about her house, she always comes back to the light. Her apartment is on the second floor, with balconies on three sides, and neighbors who wave at one another from across the way. From morning to evening, there is sunshine. When she isn't working, she loves being at home in the afternoons, getting ready for the evening meal. Her sons have their own homes now, but after they finish work, in the late afternoon, they might pass by to say hello. That's her favorite time of day.

After all of these years in this apartment, when Dora thinks of home, the first thing that comes to mind is tranquility, and the safety of home. To her, home is where you can really relax, where you don't have any worries. When she comes home after work, the first thing that she does is to sit down in her chair, perhaps to watch some television. Later in the evening, after Nino goes to bed, she stays up, enjoying that peaceful feeling.

She isn't one to change her furniture all the time. She likes things as they are and she leaves things as they are. Her home is her bubble, and its continuity soothes her. After more than three decades in her house, the kitchen is the only room that she would like to update.

. . .

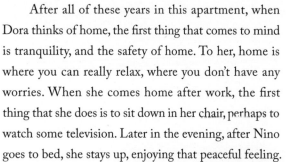

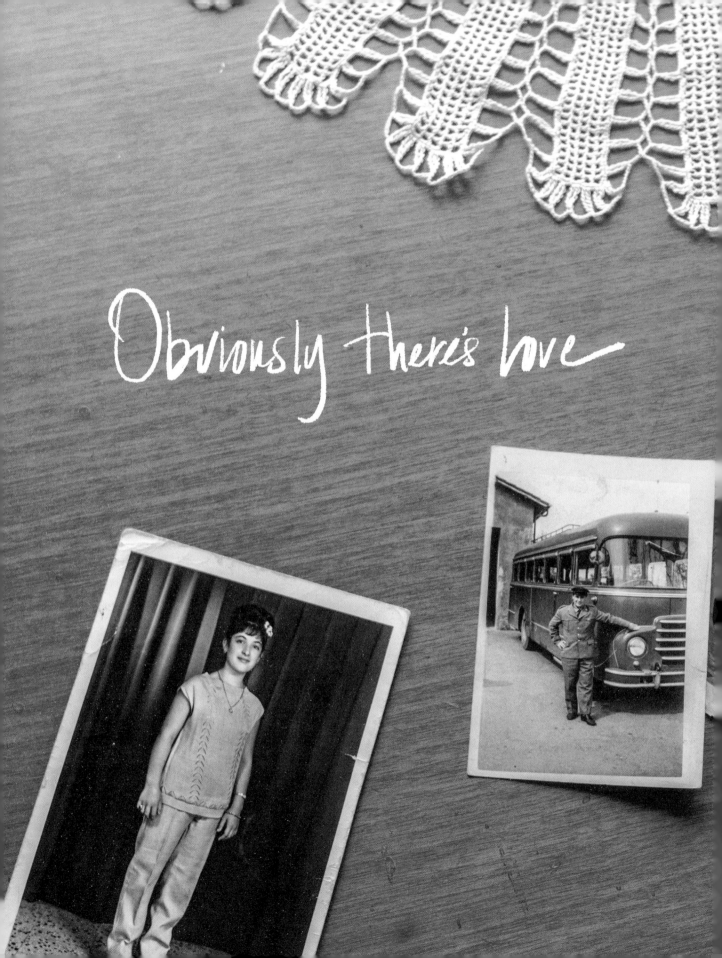

Obviously there's love

Experiencing Dora's home is like experiencing her—a rush of energy and light and warmth. She made a very big impact on our family when we were with her. She reminds me of my grandmother, warm and loving, and getting to know her was very special to us. Nate and I always talk about her, and her warmth and the pride she takes in everything she does.

When I spoke with Dora about her home, with the help of a translator, it was springtime, half a century since the spring when she first met Antonino (who goes by Nino) at an Easter lunch at a friend's house. The host was a friend of both families. She was fifteen. He was six years older. For him, she said, it was love at first sight.

They married when Dora was seventeen. It was pretty normal for two people to get married that young in Sicily, she assured me. And she chose well; they celebrated their fiftieth wedding anniversary two years ago. They have a good life together.

I asked her what the secret of their successful marriage has been. "Obviously, there's love," she said.

That's the first reason why their marriage has lasted so long. The second thing she attributes their relationship to is their differences. "We're opposites. We complement each other in some way. We acknowledge each other's differences, and we respect each other."

As she describes it, he's very easygoing and relaxed, whereas Dora is much more dynamic and impulsive, with a lot of energy. She smiles and adds that, in the beginning, Nino was very jealous and possessive. As time went by and they learned to trust each other, he became more relaxed.

Before Dora goes to bed, everything in the kitchen has to be perfect. It has to be clean, nothing out of order. And the first thing that she does when she gets up in the morning is make sure that the bed in the bedroom is perfectly made. That devotion to organization she attributes to her maternal grandmother, Maria, who raised her.

Dora is very similar to her grandmother. Because both of Dora's parents worked, they left her as a young child with her grandmother, and they only saw each other on the weekends. When Dora was seven, her parents decided to emigrate to Australia. Her younger sister moved with her parents, but Dora decided to stay with her grandmother, with whom she had a very powerful and close relationship. She also had a very powerful and close relationship with her grandmother's house. She didn't want to leave, and so she stayed.

When she was ten, she remembers, her grand-mother said, "Okay, come here. You have to learn how to iron." That was it; she had to learn how to iron. She had a very loving life that was also very strict and organized. She lived with her grandmother until she was married at seventeen, and Maria's influence still echoes in her sense of order and the way she cares for her home.

• • •

Dora and Nino had been married for fifteen years when they found this home. The first house they had lived in together as a couple, with their two sons, didn't have enough light. They also wanted to move to a quieter residential area, away from the center where there's too much traffic, too much chaos.

They saw a lot of homes and decided on this one because of the balconies, the light, and the residential area. Dora knew that she didn't want an independent house; she wanted to live in an apartment where there's life, where she could hear the neighbors. Not too much, obviously, but she wanted to know that there was always someone around. The only thing she didn't like about this home was that the kitchen was a little smaller than what she was used to. That's still the only negative thing she will say about the house.

Dora very much sees her house in terms of the present, not the past. She likes her things, and she likes coming home and recognizing everything. She has her habits, and she likes what she has around her.

2 uova
biscotti a

torta
pasta: 250 far
4 cuc
125 t
3 tu

crema
300 zucchero
4 cucchiai
4 uova in
4 bicchieri
3 limoni (

It's a
little bit
like falling
in love
with a
person

When she thinks of the past, she thinks instead about her parents' house. The home is still owned by her family, but it is painful for her to go there because it reminds her of her parents' illnesses and deaths. The house is a relic, closed and left as it was, with all the furniture inside. She's chosen to leave it there because it's too hard for her to do otherwise. Nothing has been moved. It's like a time capsule, a ghost.

Her dreams now are not about the house her parents lived in, they are about her own home. Before she dies, she wants to tear down a wall and make a bigger kitchen. That's the most important goal for her. She has two grown sons and grandchildren, and if everyone wants to cook together, they will need a bigger kitchen.

• • •

Dora's home is a happy house because of everything that's happened there and how she has felt there. She's raised two children there, and she's very proud of the way they've also started their own families. There's been happiness all around.

"Although we all have our problems, obviously," she said, "everything turns out for the better in the end." It has brought her good fortune, staying in that particular house and having that life there. "It's a little bit like falling in love with a person," she said.

Leaving now is out of the question. This is Dora's house. She's never going to give it to anyone else. Her love for her home is about her space. It's the light. It's the neighborhood. It's the neighbors who say hello to each other from the balcony. It's a lifetime.

Dancing with the Moon

FATIMA

Everyone knows Fatima as a choreographer and dancer. I know her to also be a dreamer, a spiritual goddess and a secret nature farmer. The home she lives in has been a vital part of her latest transformation.

She was on her way to a rehearsal for the Oscars when I caught her and asked her to talk with me about her relationship with her home. This prolific creator has worked with Michael and Janet Jackson, Pharrell, and so many others. One of the sexiest and most elegant people I know, Fatima exudes a "mother nature" essence at the same time. She is always going somewhere amazing and doing something incredible, and when she comes home, she enters a space that vibrates the way she vibrates. What's really beautiful is that she listens to her intuition.

For seventeen years, she lived in a home called the Château Normandy. She moved in when her son was two years old, and she stayed until he was grown enough to be on his own. When he left home, she gave herself permission to do the same thing. Her new home in Ojai has helped her find herself, and it gave me insight into the different ways that our homes keep us as we go through the phases of our lives.

The space that kept Fatima and her son for so many years was a Spanish-style home that was full of color—4,600 square feet of art and memories. It was a home full of parties and visitors, one she always cared for and tended. As she recalled, "I redecorated three times over."

When her son went away to college, she felt like she didn't have a purpose anymore. After talking to a life coach, she realized that this next phase of life offered her room to live a little more for herself.

"What do I want to do, and how do I want to do that?" she asked. She found inspiration when she was at the yurt she kept in the Santa Monica mountains, her "secret space," where she had a copper bathtub and the backdrop of nature. The whole place was a natural, out-of-the-city experience, one she shared with her then-boyfriend, Thomas.

Fatima has always been a girl who loves plants and flowers, and she was able to imagine herself living a much more peaceful, wonderful existence in the garden, hands in the dirt. Reaching out for something in nature was a path to understanding how she wanted to live the next half of her life.

Ojai, California, called to her. "You need to be here," something in her said. "You need to be in nature."

There was a house online in that area that seemed promising, but the photos were terrible. She went up to see it anyway and discovered a house like a blank canvas, waiting for her to fill it with herself. All it took was that one viewing to inspire her to buy it.

Early on, when she was in escrow, she would drive up from Los Angeles and have conversations with herself about what she was doing. "You know," she would tell herself, "you and Thomas probably aren't gonna stay together, so you're gonna have to be able to live out here by yourself. Are you okay to live out here, all the way out here by yourself?"

As she crossed into Ojai, when she got into the valley, came around, and went through the hills, the answer was screaming at her. "Yes. You're gonna be fine."

A few months after she moved in, the pandemic happened. For her, it was like the universe had plucked her out of the city and put her here. It was the time of year when the orange trees blossom, and the smell in this small city was intoxicating. She was so happy that she had listened to the call and come to Ojai.

Living in this peace, she became comfortable with being quiet and alone. Even making tea became a meditation for her. She began to really appreciate the stars and the moon. It's because she let go of the noise of the city, she feels, that her career is exploding in the best of ways.

"This place is something so special," said Fatima, talking about how magnificent it all is when the moon is full. "I have dance parties by myself. I make these playlists, and then I'll light my candles in my fireplace. Completely all alone, and you would think I was just in a nightclub, smiling and laughing and just in love with life."

All she wanted was to go home, and now she has.

• • •

When Fatima was young, her family moved every few years. She was born in Arkansas and, from the age of five, even after she moved to LA, she spent every summer in Arkansas, playing in the woods, catching lightning bugs with her cousins. Years later, when her son was young, she bought a house in Atlanta near her family, just so he could have that same experience.

Fatima's family lived in South Central, Inglewood, Hawthorne, Gardena; all over LA. They ended up in San Pedro when she was in junior high school. "And then," she said, "my Mom had the nerve to move to Corona, California, when nobody was out there. It was dust and subdivisions. I just thought my life was awful."

She used to daydream, "I know there's more out there. Has to be.' Cause San Pedro—you're at the end of the freeway." She felt like she was at the end of the world, and she had to get out. Then she realized that dance could get her out, but her mom didn't want her dancing. Looking back, Fatima describes it as a "super crazy" time in her life. Despite her mother's resistance, Fatima knew that she could travel the world with dance—and she did. She has been going, going, going since she was eighteen years old.

At nineteen, she had her first apartment, in Studio City. She promised herself that she'd have a Jeep and a loft by the time she was 21. She did that too.

"Moved downtown and had a loft and a red Jeep, and was living my Flashdance dream," she said.

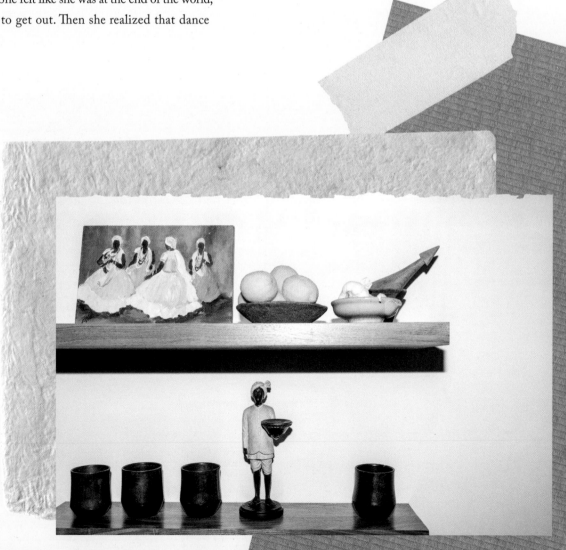

She remembers driving to clubs, taking Sunset Boulevard and checking out the homes in Los Feliz. She made another promise to herself that if she could ever afford a house, she would live there. Sure enough, at twenty-six, she was looking at a house in Los Feliz. It was the first house she ever fell in love with. The moment she walked in, she said, "Can I write an offer?" She didn't need the full tour in order to know. She just felt the energy of the house. That was enough.

Her life changed when she had a child. She wanted a forever home, a place where she could stay put, where she could see her son grow up. Château Normandy was the only home her son has known, and when she sold it, a year after moving to Ojai, he wasn't happy about it—"at first," she clarifies. For her, it was time. Everywhere she looked, there were so many memories of trips, experiences, and adventures; it was too much of her past. She didn't want the house to define her. She wanted to start anew. She took an inventory of what she needed to let go of and she had an estate sale.

"The Château Normandy needed a family to be in that house," she added. And there was someplace else that she needed to be.

• • •

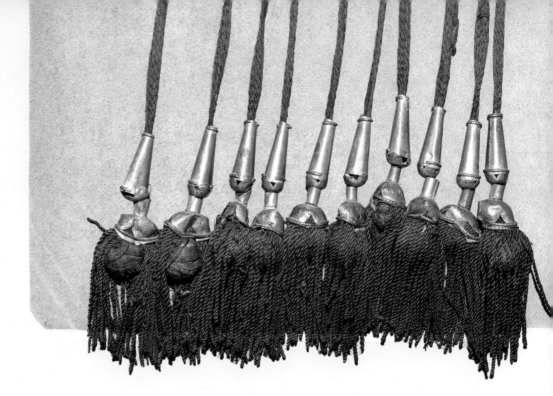

The house in Ojai already felt like a piece of her when she moved in—she just had to add some personality. She kept her art from Château Normandy, much of which she's had for twenty years. Hung on these big white walls in her Ojai house, the pieces have become unrecognizable. Her friends ask, "When'd you get that?" about things she's always had. In the old house, it was around so much color that it just blended in. In this home, all her art looks different. She can appreciate it in a different way.

Fatima is right where she wants to be. There's something magical about this valley for her, and she is softer here. "I think I have more patience," she said. "I've reprogrammed. I'm not on the same frequency. The city, you're just in it. You don't realize how much you're in it, until you step away into a place like that. It's a frequency shift and change that I needed in life."

She bought a greenhouse for the backyard, and she's been teaching herself how to landscape, making some mistakes, and buying big old olive trees as she figures it out and learns about plants. She has planted a pear tree, a pomegranate tree, a fig tree, and a plum tree; persimmon and apricot trees were already there.

Fatima has been watching all the trees start coming into bloom. She is blooming with them.

She is blooming

with them

CHAPTER ELEVEN

Legacy

POPPY AND OSKAR

My maternal grandmother Arline was an elegant, complicated, fiery Portuguese woman. Her house was simple, yet layered: plastic-lined furniture; two rocking chairs, one for her and the other for my grandfather; ceramics she had made and painted; and patchwork throws, also made by her, everywhere. My grandfather loved Westerns so there was the occasional bronze horse in their decor. It was delightfully chaotic and it all worked because it was deeply reflective of them both.

Arline had an extraordinary green thumb. Every window was lined with glass shelves lit for plants that were thriving. In her backyard there was a 1,000-square-foot greenhouse, which was supposed to be off limits—although I was often invited in with her if I didn't tell any of my cousins!

There was something surprisingly nurturing about her home for me. I say surprisingly because, based on the stories I have heard about how my grandmother conducted her relationships, I wouldn't have expected her home to be a place where I found respite. My grandmother didn't find herself as a nurturer until much later in

life, after her daughters had grown and she had become a grandmother. It was almost as if she adopted hobbies and practices that were meant to nurture and support, create and share, because those were the things she struggled with as a young woman and mother.

Her home always felt warm to me, like her. Everything about it was rooted in tenderness. Today I wonder, "Is this how she saw herself, or how she wanted to be seen?"

I think about my grandmother and her home a lot: the sounds made by the sliding door to the backyard; the smell of her quilt room, which was always ridden with cats; the kitchen table, placed perfectly in the corner under the window so she could sit and drink her coffee in her favorite spot, basking in the sunshine. And my grandmother in her kitchen, looking over it all with pride and resolve.

This is one of my first memories of the feeling of home, of warmth, of welcome. As a child, I was always dreaming about the home I would have someday. My idea of home was always a fantasy, and what I felt at my grandmother's house was a part of that.

• • •

One fantasy I have long had is one of returning to my own Portuguese roots. My mother has always talked about wanting to live in Portugal, and it has been something that has been at the back of my mind. The idea of living in a place that feels rural and disconnected from the world was interesting to me because it seemed like the complete opposite of how my family lives now. It rose up within me when I went to visit Andre at his farm. I was so inspired by his connection to the land, to the peace and purpose that he was living with. It was a feeling like the one that I had been envisioning for my family.

I shared this dream with Andre, who got it completely. He sent me a text one day: "There is a seventeenth-century farm coming available. I think this is something you should look at." It was a really special place, he told me. Old and original homes like this don't usually exist anymore because, as they fall into ruin over

the years, people want to build something modern rather than to repair and restore them.

Nate and I went that weekend to look at it. We pulled down a long dirt road a mile long just to get to the house. We walked inside, and it was a complete ruin. None of the rooms were livable. But as we walked the land, I kept thinking about everything I had learned recently from people who had seen the possibilities.

Would you like a life in balance?

The Fifth Avenue house was the first time I fell in love with a home. I knew that home would hold us and keep us. This house in Portugal could be something else: a legacy for our children. As a young gay man, the dream of having a family of my own seemed impossible. I didn't know that great love would be possible. Now, having this family, and being able, through a lot of hard work, to pass something on to them that they would always have—I never thought that I was going to be able to do that. The realization was a special moment for me.

All of this was going through my head the day we toured the home in Portugal. I was with Nate alone, so it was a unique experience because we could just be really present. Nate kept asking me if I was okay because I was so quiet. I don't think I've been that still ever in my life. It was clarity.

We made our offer that day, and when it was accepted, we were jubilant. With Fifth Avenue, I remember moving back in and knowing that the echoes of every experience we've ever had were in that house. Fifth Avenue felt like a second chance at a first love. Portugal is something else, something unexpected. When I walked into the house in Portugal for the first time after we bought it, I thought it was going to be

fireworks and confetti and cannons firing. Instead, I felt a profound sense of relief. Along with that came the realization that this feeling was calling me home.

I asked Nate about his connection to the place. "I have always spent a lot of time in Europe," he said. "I lived in France, I speak French, I've traveled a lot. I've always felt very much at home there. Some places, it feels like I've lived there before in a past life. Portugal felt like an extension of my innate comfort and serenity and joy. It felt like somebody was saying, 'Would you like a life in balance? Well, here, buy this farm.'"

To him, my joy in it only increases his. He said that, as soon as the plane landed in Portugal, he witnessed a transformation in me. "As soon as you had your wits about you in the car, five minutes outside of the airport, looking at Lisbon and the bridge connecting it to the mainland, your energy shifted in a way that was fascinating to me," he told me. "I think that the idea of the house there started to become concrete and possible and real when I watched how happy you seemed in that country."

• • •

It feels like I've

lived there before
in a past life

I had the idea to ask my mother if she wanted to move there with us and fulfill her own dream of living in Portugal. My mother is fantastic, and she's always outdone herself to give to others. She's lived a really hard life, always working three jobs to provide for our family and to survive. Now I had this opportunity to give back to her. I said to her, "What if...?"

She loved the idea. We had a beautiful conversation about it all.

The first time she saw the house was also the first time my children saw it. I couldn't believe it was all happening like this: that my mother was moving to Portugal, that she would be a part of this house for my children. All of these culminations and new beginnings still make me very emotional. Fifth Avenue is our home, and as long as we live in New York, that's where I want to be. I see this land in Portugal as being for my children. My intention is for my children to have it, and for their children to have it. Like Gibi's Venetian palace, it'll be theirs forever if they want it to be.

I asked Nate what he thinks this place means for our family, and he brought up James and Alexandra. "I watched their children grow up in this really free, international way, where they were comfortable in all of these different cultures and countries," he said. "They were welcome wherever they went because they were raised with the world as their classroom. The fact that Poppy and Oskar will grow up and say, 'We know Portugal. We live in Portugal part time. We're going back and we can't wait;' they're going to want to bring friends to the farm for a month someday...this is a

level of access that I hope becomes really important to them for their own reasons, not for ours."

In our home in New York, we have a picture of the house in Portugal in our bathroom, on the shelf above our sinks. It's one of Nate's favorite things in the house.

"I look at that every morning when I get dressed, and it reminds me that we don't have a defined future as a family—in a positive way," he said. "That we have all this freedom and flexibility. It brings me an incredible amount of peace."

• • •

The place is just perfect, even though it's not anything like I imagined. We inherited thirty sheep. Seventeen acres. Two olive orchards. Five homes that are basically unlivable ruins. The structures that exist on the land used to provide everything for the surrounding town. There's an outdoor church, with seating in a little prayer area. There's a bread house where the bakers used to make the bread for the town. Knowing that creates all these spiritual moments for me. I knew right away which house would be for my mom, who remarried. Her husband, whom I adore, makes bread. The house that I gave them is the bread house, which still has the old bread oven. It all just fits.

Are the homes my favorite houses I've ever seen? No. Will they be amazing and spectacular when we're done? Yes. I could see, within the ruins, the potential and the life. So could Nate.

I asked Nate how he feels about the prospect of working together on this place. "I can't wait to tear out everything ugly," said Nate. "I love the idea of us being in a place that has this mystical, ancient feeling. I can't imagine what it's going to be like to put a glass in a dishwasher there—the juxtaposition of living there in a simple but modern way within the confines of these ancient trees and these ancient paths and these beautiful things."

It's a lot of work, and there's going to be a lot of restoration, but I care more about what's happening outside of the house there than I do what's happening in it. That's something I never would have thought I would say. For somebody whose whole life is beholden to design, I am fascinated by the idea that I am finding

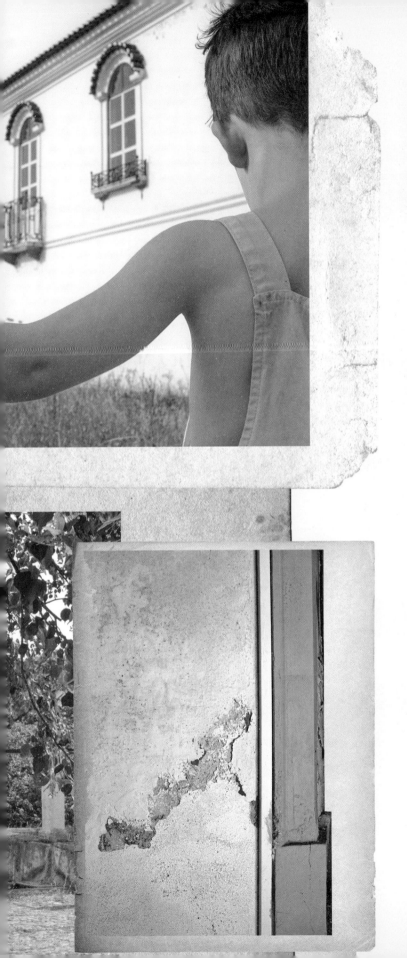

peace in a place that has little to do with it. Nate feels the same way. The priority for us right now is revitalizing the land. That's something I didn't ever think was possible. It is a different type of connection than we have been valuing, which has been a really interesting thing to figure out and to work through.

"I love that it's not about the house," Nate told me. "I love that it's about the land. I love that it's about the garden. I love that it's about nature. I feel like a custodian. I love that it feels safe. I love how rural it is. That you don't see a neighbor. I love the olive trees and the aqueducts and the ancient iron trellises and the fact that there are all these homes on the property. I love how weird it has become over the years, like the ridiculous swimming pool that's like the size of a resort in Ibiza."

When we're there, I told Nate, I loved seeing our daughter out playing with the chickens. I loved seeing our son—who's very particular, the sweetest boy in the world—being outside, getting dirty all day.

He's so excited about all the adventures they are going to have over the years. "The kids are just going to disappear and discover wells and that weird little sort of theater, church moment," said Nate. "Every time we're on the land we discover more things. Oskar will be five when the house is livable. I can't imagine being five years old and going out with a little stick and a wicker basket to pick oranges."

I love our life in New York. We live in a city where we can show up in a million ways and get out there. We have a really beautiful life in New York. Portugal is a different type of opportunity, and time will show us what it is meant to be.

There's nothing but space there. And it's ours.

Culminations

When I was growing up, my mother had a little game that she liked to play. Wherever we were, whatever we were doing, she would ask me to pause and notice something that was beautiful and talk about it. The question would snap me into consciousness and require me to be present. It opened up my eyes.

I found myself thinking about that game as I reflected on the people in this book and what they found beautiful about their homes. That feeling of being present and looking for beauty came up again and again as I learned what people loved about their homes. For Oprah, the trees. For Andre, the land. For Dora, the light. Their awareness of what they love about their spaces has snapped me into consciousness, opened up my eyes.

Walking into these homes and seeing how people live and seeing what they value—seeing ideas of home through their eyes, through their words—has changed me. Thanks to this book, I'm looking at things differently and pulling things differently and thinking about things differently. I can see so clearly the ways I have been influenced by all of the people in this book.

I think of Oprah with her trees and nature, and the dirt road and the pillars and the stars, because in Portugal, the stars at night are incredible.

I think of James and Alexandra creating that place in Mérida for themselves out of a falling-down ruin, and how they wound up providing something for their children to inherit. I've come to understand throughout this process that there are creators and there are inheritors. It made me think about the idea of legacy and consider what I wanted to create for my own children to hold.

I think about how Brooke and Michael, who have this great love in this big city, helped me fall in love with New York. Their life is intimate and special and magical and little and perfect and tailored. I met them around the same time that I met Nate, and when I saw them in their nest of a home, it showed me how you can have an intimate experience in a place as massive as New York.

I think about Marcella and Bassett, discovering that old house in Napa and dragging their children out every weekend while they fixed it up and planted grapevines—and what their children created in that space.

I think about Andre and his dedication to his farm in Portugal, about how it has softened him, and about the romance of taking a chance.

I think about Gibi, fighting to keep his ancestral home on the Grand Canal and choosing not to surrender to selling.

I think about Brian and Tracy, and their desire to stay, and their openness to find another home they love some day in the future, if that's where time takes them.

I think about Dora's awareness of her relationship with light. Because of her, I understand that my connection with Fifth Avenue is all about the light there, something that I didn't really perceive until we came back to it. I can see now that when Nate and I lived in our townhouse, which was gorgeous and in the best neighborhood in the West Village, I missed the sunlight because our home was dark. I didn't realize how much I was like a cat—how much I like to be in the light throughout the day. Dora reminded me to pay attention to that.

I think about Fatima and who she is becoming, and the gardens she is tending, and how her space nurtures her future in the way that her old house nurtured her past.

There's something so poetic about this journey. I don't think I would ever have looked at the home in Portugal the same way, had I not gone through the experience of writing this book. I wouldn't have recognized the raw beauty of it. It is beautiful, but I wouldn't have recognized the potential to live in it the way I can recognize now. That's a good twist for me. It's a big deal.

I began the intro by saying this isn't going to be a beautiful design book, but it turns out that beauty is what this book is all about—the beauty of intention and connection, perception and memory, ceremony and ritual—and most importantly, of life and love.

Acknowledgments

Writing this book—a process that unfolded over the course of two years—has been unlike anything I have ever experienced. The vulnerability was unnerving and exhilarating all at the same time. I am hooked.

When I look back at the journey of creating, I think about the incredible people who joined me on the path to completion. To them I say, thank you. The freedom I had to be present throughout is in large part because of you.

Kelsey Berlacher and Libby Bush, my dearest friends and managers, were there to champion a dream and fight to make it a reality.

Jan Miller, one of the most spectacular women I have met, took that dream and found a publisher in HarperCollins that believed in what I had to say, and has always believed in me herself. Thank you Lynne Yeamans and Marta Schooler for such beautiful stewardship and efforts toward protecting everything this book is to me. Joan Wong, thank you for helping bring this vision to life.

Paige McKinney and Julie Horowitz helped orchestrate and organize and facilitate scheduling and shooting a book that stretched across the globe, during Covid and numerous other complications. They listened to me read excerpts of the book throughout and cried along with me on the floor of my office. Their grace, patience, and resilience are unparalleled.

Lauryn Tumpkin and Courtney Paul threw themselves into the creative process of this book and navigated my often very "particular" perspective. The gift of seeing the world through their eyes, watching them meet the people in the book, and learning their stories, will always be one of my most cherished experiences.

Sandra Bark, author, secret romantic, and now, friend. She took ideas, fears, joy, confusion, passion, exploration, love and helped me craft the words to make this book a reality. She moves through the world with passion and an acute awareness of what really matters. The gift of her writing has changed the way I see design and shifted how I see the world.

And to my mother, Gwen. She always told me to dream, always taught me to chase beauty, always believed I had something to say. Thank you for giving me the confidence to believe.

HarperCollins books may be purchased for educational,
business, or sales promotional use.
For information, please email the Special Markets Department
at SPsales@harpercollins.com.

FIRST EDITION

Interior photographs on pages 26–27 (bedroom, center) and
29 (background photo) © Kelly Marshall/Architectural Digest

Designed by Joan Wong

Library of Congress Control Number: 2022950277
ISBN 978-0-06-320610-6

23 24 25 26 27 IMG 10 9 8 7 6 5 4 3 2 1